GW00363456

Country Ways

A Taste of the Country in Hampshire & Dorset

Also available:

Country Ways
A Taste of the Country in Kent & Sussex

Country Ways

A Taste of the Country in Hampshire & Dorset

ANTHONY HOWARD

Countryside Books/TVS

Country Ways
is produced for TVS by
COUNTRYWIDE FILMS LTD.

First Published 1990
© Text Anthony Howard 1990

All rights reserved.
No reproduction permitted
without the prior consent
of the publishers:

Countryside Books
3 Catherine Road
Newbury, Berkshire

ISBN 85306 094 1

Front Cover Photograph by Mike Read (Swift Picture Library Ltd.)
Back Cover Photograph by Andy Williams

Black and white photographs by Tom Howard
Line drawings by Pip Challenger

Colour Photographs:
Michael J. Allen (Swift Picture Library Ltd.) p72
Robin Fletcher (Swift Picture Library Ltd.) p71
Terry Heathcote pp18, 36, 53, 54
Mike Read (Swift Picture Library Ltd.) p17
Andy Williams p35

Produced through MRM Associates Ltd, Reading
Typeset by Acorn Bookwork, Salisbury
Printed in England by Borcombe Printers, Romsey

CONTENTS

1 Milton Abbas
and the Melcombes   9

2 Beaulieu Heath   21

3 The Teffonts   31

4 The Melburys   43

5 Weyhill   55

6 The Chalke Valley   64

7 Pamber Forest   75

8 The Cerne Valley   84

9 The Winterslows   94

INTRODUCTION

There is still a serenity in much of the central part of the South of England. Hampshire, with its open farmland and wooded slopes; Dorset and its blue-misted valleys and ancient hamlets; and Wiltshire and Berkshire with their green downland and clear skies all have much good countryside that is still worth loving and cherishing. It is less noisy and turbulent here than in the south-east corner with the Channel Tunnel, the M25 and Gatwick Airport. And in these privileged counties live some of the luckiest people on earth, surrounded by thatched villages, calm rivers and rich soils.

At his best, man is a sensitive and civilised preserver of nature and wildlife. At his worst, he is the greatest destroyer of all. In a world which shelters hundreds of millions of people more than it should be asked to, it is becoming increasingly important for people to treat the forests and hills, the rivers and the oceans, the valleys and the skies with kindness, compassion and concern. Otherwise, one day, Nature will disown the human race. And who will argue that the earth would not be a far kinder, calmer and cleaner place without the greed and hatred and carelessness of human beings?

In Dorset and Hampshire and their neighbouring counties there are still hopeful signs that the future can produce cleaner countryside than the past has done. It is up to the people of the counties – and the thousands who visit and pass through – to treat them and their scenery and wildlife with the love and respect which they deserve and which, for far too long, they have been denied.

MILTON ABBAS
AND THE MELCOMBES

MILTON Abbas, which stands in a deep valley to the south-west of Blandford Forum and amongst the chalk hills of Dorset, is one of the county's show-pieces. In the 1770s the Earl of Dorchester had a magnificent new house built beside the mediaeval abbey from which the village takes its name. He failed to realise though that his view of the wooded countryside would be spoilt by the cottages of the village. So, in the democratic way of those times, he destroyed Milton Abbas and rebuilt it in its present form with the addition of a lake – presumably to try to soften the blow for the homeless villagers. It stands today like a charming, thatched Toytown and is much admired by tourists and trippers – though not in the cold weeks of December.

In the shadow of nearby Bulbarrow Hill, with its views across the Blackmore Vale, lie the Melcombe villages, which have been there since Domesday, changing their names with the aristocratic families which owned them in turn. In old English Melcombe means Meoluc-cumb – the fertile valley of milk. And this is still, over the centuries, notable cow country. It also carries all the splendour and beauty of Dorset, the forgotten county, and even in a bleak December week, there is here some of the best countryside which the West Country has to offer.

IN spite of his size, Percy the pet pig sometimes still spends the night inside Long Ash Cottage at Milton Abbas. He is owned and cared for by farmer's wife, Maureen Case, who also has one of the finest collections of rare breeds of hens and bantams in the country. Sally, her pet parrot, sometimes thinks that she might be one of their almost equally colourful number; 'Sally is a scarlet macaw. We've had her for nearly fifteen years. She belonged to some people we knew who had a restaurant. They couldn't keep all their birds so, somehow or other, I seemed to get landed with Sally. I wouldn't be without her for the world now. She's such wonderful company. Oscar, her friend, is a white cockatoo. We've only had him about two years. He's very affectionate but dreadfully noisy. It's like living in the front room with a donkey. Very destructive too. Takes lumps out of the furniture if you turn your back on him. He belonged to some other friends who simply couldn't stand the noise. They couldn't decide what to do with him, so he finished up here with me of course. As for Percy the pet pig, we have two young Berkshire sows you see. When they had their first litters, one of them decided she didn't like her piglets at all and went for them. So the other one had to bring up both families. In all the upheaval and messing around which that involved, poor little Percy got badly trodden on. In fact I thought

Farmer's wife Maureen Case with Sally, her pet scarlet macaw. She also keeps a fine collection of rare breeds of hens and bantams on the farm under the shadow of nearby Bulbarrow Hill.

he was dead. So we brought him into the house and got up in the middle of the night to feed him and, of course, he grew. He practically lived in the house. He stays out most of the time now because he's so big. But he used to be just like the dogs. He'd lie in front of the fire and even open the oven door if he wasn't warm enough. He's lovely, though he's getting too big for it now, which is sad. But he can't help being big, can he?'

Maureen is a slim, enthusiastic woman, full of energy and always on the go. Today, she and her husband have turned what was their hobby into The Rare Poultry, Pig and Plant Centre with over thirty breeds of poultry and all the rare breeds of pigs including, of course, Percy. But it is the sound of the cockerels, hens and bantams which overwhelms everything else at Long Ash Cottage. Maureen comes out with two tiny and beautiful birds in her arms; 'These are called Belgian D'Anvers. They're the smallest breed I keep. They're sweet things. One is a blue quail and the other is a silver. They have the same neat feather pattern except where one is blue, the other is black, white, buff and a bit of blue as well. The feather pattern on one of them is a bit muddly on the wings. They're both quite nice in the hackle. Good, neat heads and, of course, D'Anvers should have lovely beards and side-whiskers. They're also quiet little birds, not that it would matter too much out here. We're well isolated. I come from about fifteen miles the other side of Bulbarrow. But I've been here nearly 25 years now so I think probably I'm a local. It's a great part of the country. We're far enough away from what passes as a main road to escape the traffic. No neighbours luckily for the birds to disturb, which is a big boon. Lots of our poultry friends have trouble with birds crowing and complaints from local people who get woken up. It's a very rural area. Beautiful woodland, especially if you like walking or riding. A lot of wildlife, including quite a few deer, which I often see when I'm out in the woods. It's surprising how close you can get to them, particularly when you're on a horse. They take no notice of you then.'

On a table in her garden under the pale blue winter sky Maureen is washing, shampooing and drying with a soft towel a dramatically sleek black bird with long, pheasant's tail feathers and eagle eyes. Anybody who thinks that hens hate water would not believe the scene because this one seems to be relishing its beauty bath; 'She's a black Sumatra hen and you have to do this before you take them to a show. She's quite used to it and, yes, I believe she enjoys it. Make sure their feet are clean before you start or the water gets dirty instantly. Use a mild shampoo or even better, if you're worried about it, a baby shampoo, so that if it gets in their eyes it won't hurt them. It's very important to rinse them thoroughly afterwards, otherwise the feathers get clogged up with soap. Then they won't look good when you've finished. It's amazing the difference it makes. A bird can look quite presentable, but you give her a bath and she's transformed – feathers so much fluffier and generally cleaner and better all round. People think that hens and water don't mix and the birds do get a bit of a shock when you start off for the first time. They struggle and water spills everywhere and there's a mess. But they learn quickly. People don't give hens enough credit. They think they're stupid creatures. But as soon as they become individuals and they get used to being handled, they're not frightened any more. In fact some of them thoroughly enjoy it. This one – the Sumatra Game Hen – she's a true professional. She's about five years old now. She's won lots of prizes and she just loves it. She talks to me all the time in her own way as long as the water's warm.'

With a deft flick of her arm Maureen wraps the soaking bird in a towel until only its beady eyes and beak are showing. Then she goes inside to give it a warm beside the Raeburn; 'I think I probably prefer birds and animals to people. They're very loyal. They don't ask much of you. All they need is to be cared for, to be well-loved, well-fed and looked after. Most humans demand a great deal more than that.'

CHARLIE Hardy was born and bred in Melcombe Bingham and has never wanted to stray far from his thatched Sycamore Cottage. He spends much of his time now in a builder's yard at next-door Ansty, where he keeps things tidy and shipshape and remembers his young days in the nearby villages; 'We come to live with the village proper when I wasn't quite three. My father had just died and that was 74 year ago now. The village hasn't changed at all you know – not in that time really. A couple of the houses have fell down, but nothing very much. When we were kids, up where I did live, there used to be a cottage that has fell down now. And there used to be another one along there and an old man and his daughter used to live in it. And every night he did go to bed, going on about half-past eight that was, and he used to say his prayers. And 'twas out loud you know. Everybody could hear him, even out in the road they could. And his daughter used to say to we boys, "Hark to the old liar up there. Go outside and fling some stones onto the tin roof." 'Cos when the roof did leak he couldn't afford to put no more thatch on, so he did put a piece of galvanised up. And we kids used to run out and grab stones up off the road and fling them up onto the roof. And he used to shout out to his daughter, "You go and shift they boys. They be throwing them stones up onto my galvanised on the roof." Course, this used to tickle us and we ran off laughing.'

Charlie is pure Dorset. His family is said to be related to the great Dorset wordsmith, Thomas Hardy, though on the wrong side of the blanket. Great authors feel that they have the excuse for their sins of needing to provide vivid material for their fiction. Even in the last quarter of the twentieth century, Charles would fit immaculately into the great stories which his forefather wrote; 'The barn that I do most of my work in was part of a brewery. It was where the malt was made. They used to have the barley in here and spread it out. 'Twas heated and then they used to have ploughs, wooden ploughs, and a man used to bide here and push the plough up and down through the barley, turning it over. Outside, they used to have a tin shed and, in there, they used to make the lemonade. And when we were kids we used to pop down – might be half-a-dozen, sometimes there were a dozen of us – and we'd go up to the old man that was making the lemonade and we'd say, "A bottle of lemonade, Mr Gilbert?" He'd say, "You know me, sonny. You pop back up the shop and gid I a half-ounce of baccer for me pipe and I'll see what I can do." Course, we kids used to run back up the shop. Well, it's about nearly half-a-mile back up in the village. We'd get his baccer and come back down. Then we did all have a bottle of lemonade – don't matter how many 'twas. Of course, we were satisfied then. Till the next time when we did come down. But we did still get our bottle of lemonade.'

Charlie sits in his draughty shed making wooden pegs for marking out foundations on building sites. Elsewhere he chips the concrete off old bricks and stacks them in tidy piles. In a building across the way he oils piles of metal clips, which are used for holding scaffolding together. His movements are slow but he is economical with his strength and every action is measured and meticulous. Every now and then he trundles an old wheelbarrow full of wood chippings down to a fire which smoulders softly at the bottom of the yard; 'We had to make our own pleasure them times, you know. All sorts we used to get up to. Not like now when it's all provided. As for this job, it's quite all right. It's good for a pensioner you know. Somebody's got to keep you moving, getting about. I don't like sitting down very much. You know, not doing anything. I had more than thirty year on timber-felling before and we used to go all over the place – as far away as Yeovil or Sherborne. But I was always happy to come back to the village. It's about the best part of Dorset this. Doesn't matter what the season. You can always find something to do around here no matter what time of the year it is. It isn't very often we get snowed in or anything, wintertime. Only a couple of times. And not too bad. Though 1962 and '63 was the worst and we was snowed up proper then. The roads out of the village were blocked for three weeks. And one place just going up out of the village, when they dug the snow out where it was going right over the top, they measured it and it were 32 feet deep. That was where the snow had blowed up over the road.'

LIKE Maureen Case with her rare breeds of poultry, Dulcie House has a parrot at her home at Catherine's Well on the top of the hill in Milton Abbas. This is a green bird and it watches Dulcie keenly as she makes her tea on a cold December evening. Dulcie, among many other things is in charge of the village choir and, with Christmas approaching, that means carol-singing in the old village streets; 'We're loyal to our own parish, so the members of the choir are all Milton Abbas people. When we started the church choir we agreed to stay within our own boundaries. And the other parishes do the same. The choristers can be of any age. We welcome anyone that's really interested in singing. Christmas is naturally a special time of year but we try to do things at other times too. At harvest time and at Easter we sing special concerts. The members are disciplined. They turn up to practise every Friday evening at 7.30. They come very regular. At this time of year we sing all the normal carols that everybody knows. But we do sing a few Dorset carols which we started to learn last year. We're all very pleased with them. Being a Dorset parish, we should sing them and they're popular too. I've got several roles in the village. I'm the church organist and so I have the support of the church choir. Give me great courage they do. I'm also choir mistress and I take the Sunday School as well, which in turn leads into a recorder group. So one thing supports another. And they're all very good and the co-operation of the children's parents is remarkable. They're wonderful really.'

Holding hurricane lamps high on poles, a group of about twenty quietly walks down the high street of the village. The children are there with recorders at the ready. Everybody is well wrapped against the chill of a dark December night. One of the singers leads a donkey to add even greater charm to the scene. The solid, identical thatched houses stand back from the road with trim grass patches in front of them. A small boy knocks firmly on a front door, which opens to reveal a warm fire, a Christmas tree and sparkling decorations. A father and his daughter stand in the doorway to enjoy the singing; 'It's a lovely, old village with its thatched roofs and smoking chimneys – sort of made for carol singers. Our special songs this evening are the Dorset carol and *Little Donkey*, which the children will be playing on their recorders. The Dorset song comes from Winterbourne Zelston – just across country from here. It's about the shepherds feeding their flocks. As for *Little Donkey* we're so lucky that Mrs Raymond has brought her donkey along. He's a good addition to the choir. Once the children start playing I'm sure the donkey will want to join in. We all love this place. I've always lived in Dorset. I was born and bred here. I've been in Milton for 24 years now. I love it. I really do. And I always have done.'

As the recorders start to play, raggedly at first but then with growing confidence, somebody gives the donkey a mince pie, which it struggles to eat and then spits out with distaste. Soon the voices of the singers join the musicians in the old Christmas songs.

WHEN Rosie, the donkey in question, is not helping with the carol-singing, she lives with her friends and relatives in the care of Sheila Raymond on the hill above Milton Abbas. Sheila is a fanatic about donkeys and dogs and all her animals receive plenty of tender, loving care; 'I thought Rosie did very well at the carols. She enjoyed it. She loves to be the centre of everything. She wasn't too keen on that mince pie though; thought it was very sticky. She sloshed it all round herself and on her halter. And, as soon as I got her back to the stable, she got very self-important and kicked and bit all the other donkeys that she could see. Then, half-an-hour later when I went back, she was fast asleep in the stable absolutely worn out. If I'd brought one of the other donkeys along instead of Rosie, it would certainly have joined in the singing. Ferdy, the big black boy, he's got a tremendous voice. Anything musical and off he goes. But I thought I'd better not bring him or he'd have drowned out the children. I'm not sure he'd have added to the beauty of the singing either.'

Sheila is a small, robust, determined woman, who seems to live for her animals. Much of her day is spent with them — grooming, feeding, cleaning and caring for them; 'This is the life I have chosen. I've only lived in Milton Abbas for eleven years now. But I live in the middle of the view that I used to see from the farm where I was before, down the bottom of Bulbarrow. So I came up here and I love it. It's a perfect place to live. I'm very happy here and there are plenty of good people. We're all friendly and cheerful together. And I don't think I would like to live anywhere else because Dorset is such a lovely county wherever you go in it. Milton Abbas is the jewel in its crown. As for the donkeys, it's hard to explain why, but everybody loves a donkey and I always have too. I had a riding accident when I was young and I knew I couldn't ride again. So that's why I started to have a donkey. The nearest thing I could find to a horse, I suppose. Then it sort of grew on me. I show them — and that's terrific fun and I breed them too. I have the local mentally-handicapped children over several times a year and they ride them. The donkeys are very good with them and give them such a lot. I take them to fetes too and give donkey-rides. They're such personalities — far more so than horses. Definitely more than people too. And they really use their heads. I've got one, Penny, she'll open any bolt, any latch. It doesn't take her long. She comes and looks at it, sums it up and half-an-hour

14

Sheila Raymond with two of her large family of donkeys. Their gentle nature ensures their popularity with the many handicapped children who come to ride them.

later the gate is open and everybody else is streaming up the lane.'

In every sense, Sheila's animals are her family. And affection is given and received. As the donkeys trot down the narrow, Dorset lane beside Sheila's cottage on their way to the meadow where they spend their days, they stop every few paces to snatch something tasty from the hedges on either side; 'We all know one another well. At a show I can always recognise my donkeys' voices, even if there are lots of others there all braying like mad. They really are like people in some ways. For instance, Rosie comes indoors. If the weather is warm and I leave the door open she quite happily gets inside. The other day she came into the kitchen and took my toast, which I was having for breakfast, off the table. She left my boiled egg, which was kind of her. Sometimes she fancies a vase of flowers. She just lifts them out and leaves me with water dripping everywhere. Then, when I was bringing her to the carols, she came along very obediently even though it was pitch dark. Everything was fine until we reached the white lines across the lane where it joins the road. She thought those lines were highly dangerous and she showed, quite clearly, that she was not going to cross them. So I turned her to come home and then quickly pushed her backwards and she was across before she realised it. After that, she was happy. The moment she saw the Christmas lights and the children and the movement I could hardly keep up with her. She was trotting off down the road and she enjoyed it because she loves children. I'd recommend donkeys to anybody as long as they can find an acre of land for grazing and a shelter of some kind. They must have cover because they don't shake off rain like horses and cattle. It penetrates their soft coats. So you must never never put a donkey out in a field where there's not a stable of some kind. They're excellent for company, but not on their own. They need companionship as well. They're much better in twos.'

When she reaches the meadow Rosie goes and looks disdainfully at two glossy horses in the next field. Then she chooses a muddy patch and rolls contentedly in it for a couple of minutes. In the sky above a big buzzard flies in smooth circles searching for prey.

TOM Hibberd is 77 and knows the woods and forests of the area like the back of his hand. Before becoming a woodsman, he was in the Navy and when he was stationed at nearby Portland, he explored Dorset on his bicycle; 'I was in a place where there was no canteen, no recreational facilities at all. If you wanted a pint of beer you had to climb up the hill. So I got a bit bored and fed up with it and got myself a pushbike. From 1936 to 1939 there wasn't a village in Dorset I didn't visit. My recorded mileage was just over 90,000, though I'll certainly have done more than that. And only one lot of punctures, which was caused by a hedgehog about 3 o'clock in the morning coming down from Blandford. I ran over him in the dark and there were 27 holes in the tube. I covered them all with two patches, working by feel. In those days, if your wheels weren't turning, your lights didn't work. In my travels there was no plan or set pattern. It was a case of head towards Dorchester, go left,

16

A pearl-bordered fritillary on a dandelion: 'I only ask to be free. The butterflies are free. Mankind will surely not deny to Harold Skimpole what it concedes to the butterflies.' *Charles Dickens*

It is easy to take kestrels for granted, so many there are hovering over small animal corpses on main roads and motorways. But they are proud hawks, beautiful and ferocious hunters – and, in flight, as dramatic as any bird in the sky.

first right, first left again, second right, and I'd just wander off like that. I often found the best places by getting lost.'

Deep in the woods Tom walks in silence with a saw over his shoulder and a stick in his hand. The banks are steep here and, in the glade below the trees, a young deer lifts its head to watch him pass. It is unafraid and soon continues to graze. There is a winter hush in the trees, the birds are still and the only sound is the crunch and crackle of the man's feet as they tread down on the mud and the twigs along the path; 'I was always interested in forestry. My father was a gardener, so I suppose it comes from there. I believe there was a farmer in the family about 1700 at Chippenham in Wiltshire. Certainly, there was a cabinet-maker. So wood must be in the blood. This patch of forest near Milton Abbas was started on March 26, 1956. We came down here then and marked some of the old trees for firewood. When the lady who owned it died it was sold to a timber merchant. So then all the big trees that were any good were cut. And there was some big ones, I can tell you. Just near here there were some Douglas Fir – only planted in 1919 – but they were more than 135 feet tall. They wasn't all that thick though. Douglas never are. But they grew terrifically high and were good timber. So in March 1956 there were tree-tops and rubbish everywhere. And there was a planting order by the Forestry Commission for four years work. The agent was an ex-teak man from the colonies. We didn't plant any ash because there was plenty of it here already. But we planted a mixture. The fir-trees we put in as an early crop. That was the bread and butter. We planted some sycamore and plenty of beech too, which was the main crop. Because this is beech country without a doubt. And that's the jam. You can harvest that in a hundred years – it doesn't happen quickly. It's the kind of thing you grow if you're looking out for grandsons and great-grandsons. I reckon this lot must have cost well over £100,000 to plant. It's not the best land for growing because it's chalk and clay and the air can't get into the ground. You can see the way it sticks to your feet. But I've seen worse.'

Tom takes his saw from his back and swiftly cuts two Christmas trees – one for himself and one for a member of his family. He hoists them onto his back and, in spite of his nearly 80 years, strides strongly homewards. In the shed beside his house are stacks of beautifully turned wooden plates and bowls; 'I've always been interested in wood-turning and wood-work in general. I've never had much of an opportunity because there wasn't a lot of time and a lathe was expensive. But I was given a lesson or two a few years back and now I fiddle around when I have the chance. I don't go out and buy wood. I use firewood or whatever comes to hand. I wait for opportunities to come my way. You can always find an interesting bit of wood if you keep your eyes open. My ambition at the moment is to get something turned in wood from every estate I've worked on and that's giving me quite a few problems.'

BY most people's standards this would be spring and summer country with healthy walking, wildlife galore and gallons of fresh air. But if you like solitude and the splendour of the South Country undisturbed by human beings, perhaps, with an extra overcoat, you may find everything you want in these Dorset hills during the run-up to Christmas and the New Year. In any case, one thing you will be sure of is a warm welcome in the pubs and homes of the little villages along your way.

BEAULIEU HEATH

BEAULIEU Heath, in the heart of Hampshire's New Forest, can trace its name back to King John and the early years of the thirteenth century. When the king gave it to the Cistercian monks, Beaulieu was described as 'a fine place belonging to the king'. Bellus Locus – 'a fine place' in Latin – became Beau Lieu in the monks' French, and thus Beaulieu today.

There are those who disdain the New Forest's heathland with its thin soils and gorse, heather and bracken. But there is nowhere else like it in the South of England, and you have to travel as far west as Exmoor and Dartmoor before you find anything comparable. It is something of a miracle that it has survived so long in its present wild and lovely state, surrounded as it is by Southampton to the east and Bournemouth to the west and with London less than two hours to the north-east.

The real foresters – those whose families go back through the generations – are a shrinking breed, but their determination to retain what is best of their beloved territory remains undiminished. There are thin pickings on this poor land and there are few, if any, rich commoners. Greed for wealth is not their motive. Greed for independence, solitude and the splendour of their surroundings may be.

ONE animal which you will not see out loose on the New Forest is a goat – unless it has escaped from its meadow. Goats do too much damage to young trees and shrubs, already nibbled by deer and ponies. But at Broomhills Farm, East Boldre, Mavis Trollope keeps a mixed herd of these charming and mischievous creatures. She sells their milk locally and uses their hair to make jumpers. With two pigs, two calves, some orphan lambs and a mass of exotic birds, Mavis's life is fully occupied by her demanding family of animals; 'I was born in the forest and spent all my life here. My father did too and my grandfather before that, so we're the third generation. There's no doubt about our liking the forest. But that's not the point really. It's a good life as long as you like animals and you must also like work. It's seven days a week. It's twenty-four hours in the day and it's fifty-two weeks in the year. I wouldn't be anywhere else. I'm perfectly happy. But then I'm fond of the animals.'

The yard behind the small cottage is a jumble of huts, sheds, stables and animals of all shapes and sizes. Mavis oversees them with calm and kindness. In the meadow the goats graze peacefully while they keep a watchful eye on the gate in case their mistress might come by with some food or just to say 'hello'. In a sty at the bottom of the yard two healthy young pigs snort and rootle in the straw while a bunch of orphan lambs scamper about, hopping, skipping and playing games together. When they see Mavis approaching with their bottles of warm goats' milk they make a

Third generation forester Mavis Trollope keeps goats on her smallholding at East Boldre. Their milk is popular with local people, and their hair makes excellent wool, hand spun by Mavis.

concerted dash towards her and besiege her with their pleading eyes. It is like a scene from a peasant's farm in the Middle Ages transferred to the back end of the twentieth century. And, when Mavis sets up her spinning-wheel beside a straw bale and starts busily making balls of rich wool for clothes for her family and herself, the illusion is nearly complete; 'It's a shame that there's not very many of these smallholdings left. Because back into history they've been the backbone of the forest. When I was a child practically every house down along here had a cow. They had a pig – they had two pigs as a matter of fact. One was killed off at Christmas time. We had no electricity of course so that used to be salted, smoked and made into bacon. And the other one was always sold. That used to pay the rent, that one did. We had our own cow then. We used to make butter and cream too. They say to you now that you shouldn't have butter and that you shouldn't have cream. But I've had it all my life and I'm still alive. And it's sad because I think that all the way down along this part there's only three of these little farms left. It was different when I was a child. We all helped each other then. It was a friendly life and you did good turns. It was hard work but if you were out on the heath to get your cattle in (because they all went out then), and if you saw your neighbour's there too and they needed fetching in you'd bring them all home together. Six or a dozen it might be of an evening and, as you got near home, each cow would separate and go down a different lane to its own home. And that's how we helped each other them days. But they've gone now for good I'm afraid.'

Mavis has a sturdy, lined face which softens as she remembers the old days. She is a strong woman, confident in her strength and in her great abilities. It is doubtful whether our softer, more selfish age will breed such people. In a century from now they may no longer exist – as extinct as so many other precious species. How very much poorer this nation will be as a result.

JEFF Kitcher comes from one of the best known Beaulieu families. His house is at Furzey lane, Beaulieu, and he has recently been appointed as a Verderer. Now he has a responsibility for the Commoners' animals on the forest and for the enforcing of forest laws. To earn his living, Jeff runs a thriving timber business; 'People say my family name's one of the oldest in the forest. Must be something in it, I should say. Certainly it goes back a hundred or two years and more. And I don't think I'm the first Verderer to carry the name either. What we mainly have to do is to see to the bye-laws on the forest and to help run the whole area as smoothly as possible. We have to help the Commoners, who have rights out here, mainly based on the property they own. Between us we try and protect those rights. Then, after us, there's the Agisters. They're the policemen of the forest, who see that the cattle and ponies are all in order and healthy. We're more like the magistrates. We're needed because there's lots of pressures on the land here. Each month we've got people coming along for little bits of ground for this and that. We often have to say no, which means that we're thought of as a bit bloody-minded. But, if we didn't refuse, quite soon there'd be no forest left. Everybody always thinks that their bit is important and what they want to do with it. But they don't remember that there's thousands more thinking the same. It's hard work keeping the forest as it is, let alone trying to improve it a bit.'

Jeff rides out from his cottage at dawn to look over his ponies. He is a tall, thin, hard man, who sits high in the saddle as he canters through the gorse and splashes over the marshy heathland. His clothes are for working, not for show, and he is a workaday rider, not a weekend pleasure parader. His hands are strong on the reins and his horse is in no doubt about who is in charge; 'I've never tried anything but this and I've never wanted to. I suppose, as I've always lived here, I don't appreciate it like people from outside. But it's a good place right enough. There's the people and the freedom and the way of life. I get fed up with it sometimes but, all in all, I wouldn't want to change it. Most Commoners like me, who've been here all our lives, they've had to struggle along up to recent years. We've been bottom of the pile really. That's made us rather independent and a bit stubborn perhaps. Certainly very different from the newcomers. We're sometimes not too pleased with them. They're all right as long as they don't interfere. People buy property in the forest and, as soon as they're here, they try to tell us how to run things. I don't know how the forest existed for 900 years with just us Commoners here. According to them it hasn't, because we don't do nothing right. So they're a bit of a problem at times. They just don't understand us or the area. It's as simple and basic as that, I suppose. You see, the actual landscape of the place hasn't changed a lot in a thousand years. But the way we do things has changed a bit. The same as everything else, it moves on. The trick is to hang on to the best of the old and to make the most of the new.'

Out in the woods Jeff dons a hard hat and, chain-saw in hand, he walks into a tall stand of pine trees to start work. Down a ride a tractor carries before it a mechanical monster, which grabs the felled trees, strips the branches off them and cuts them into exact lengths; 'I would say that the forestry people do quite a lot to maintain the forest. Whatever you do in a place like this is going to cause arguments. And the Forestry Commission, for instance, they've got to pay their way and to have a little reward for their work. It's sad in a way that this job has got so industrialised. It must have been great with just saws and axes and horses and ropes. But it's progress too. That machine on the tractor does the work of three or four men I suppose. It's a strange thing but you've got a job to find blokes today, who will cut timber and that sort of thing. Younger fellows just don't want it. Too much like hard work perhaps. And then, it's like everything else today, we've got to keep our labour costs down so that we can compete with the big boys. In ten years time there'll be fir plantations, I should say, where you'll most probably have a job to see a bloke with a power-saw anywhere. It will be that mechanised. But whatever it's going to be like, I can still go home at the end of the day, all winds and all weathers, get on my horse and ride out across the forest. And that's what I enjoy best. He knows the area better than I do, that pony. If you buy one from outside and ride it on the forest you'll find him falling

24

into holes and all that sort of thing. But the local ponies get used to the place from the time they're born. When you're rounding up cows or other horses he knows what he's got to do. I suppose it's the same as with the cowboys with their horses rounding up cattle in the films. The forest ponies get like them and, you know, they're better than us after a while.'

The closest that you can get to the Wild West in Britain is the New Forest in the autumn when the pony drifts are in full swing. If you choose the right place on the right day, you can see up to a hundred horses in full flight across the heath, pursued by a score of Commoners on their ponies. These annual round-ups mean that all New Forest horses can be checked, branded and counted before the winter arrives in earnest.

PALACE House at Beaulieu is internationally known for its Motor Museum and its playgrounds. It is one of those graceful, stately homes, which has had to come to terms with the financial realities of the age. Behind the razzamatazz, the grounds and gardens of Palace House are kept in apple-pie order by a dedicated team of gardeners. One of them is Walter Elsworth, who has been working on the estate since he was sixteen. His home is at Lodge Cottage in Beaulieu, and he finds work to do there – and at the big house – even on the soggiest April day; 'April is a funny month. You get days like this sometimes when it could still be January. But you can still feel that spring's in the air. Obviously, we all like gardening when it's fine. You've got no choice though. You've got to do it when it's wet as well, because the job's still got to be done. I had a friend who worked on the estate at Exbury, where they grow all those wonderful azaleas and rhododendrons. He said that, working on an estate, you had two freedoms you had to consider. There was freedom from and freedom to. Working like I do you have freedom from the rat race, from pressures and from the hurly-burly of industry. If you work outside it's the other way round. You've got freedom to do what you want and to go where you like. It's as easy as that. That was his idea of the two freedoms. As for me, I've made my choice. I prefer what I've got and I wouldn't swap it. It could be termed a lazy man's way of life, but it's still very good for me and I'm pleased with it.'

There is nothing in the least bit lazy about Walter as he mounts his venerable bike and rides to work through the soaking streets of Beaulieu. As he crosses the bridge over the river, two great white swans drift in to land on the water. He lets himself into the Palace House grounds through one of the private entrances and is soon hard at work digging up hyacinths in one of the borders; 'I started here on the estate when I was sixteen after doing a couple of other jobs first. I followed my brother as a matter of fact. He was called up at eighteen so there was a vacancy and I followed in his footsteps. I learnt my gardening first of all from my father. He was a keen gardener. When I left school and started down here, I did two or three years with the old Head Gardener 'til I reached eighteen and was called up as well. After I'd done my soldiering, I went away from gardening for a while. I went down to the river and had about eight years down there. After that, I was on to the building staff. Then came back into the gardens about twenty-four years ago. But I'd kept in touch with it all along. The trouble is, when you work here all the time, that you tend to regard it as your own garden. That's sometimes appreciated and sometimes it's not. But I always work here and do things exactly the same as I would in my own patch.'

Walter is a strong, stocky figure with a calm and honest face, well tanned even before the first of the summer sun. He works steadily and methodically, having the wisdom to know that he will achieve more in that way; 'This is the time of year for taking out the hyacinths to dry them off and store them and getting ready to put in the begonias, which follow them. It's a changeover time really. Your spring bedding is going and you're getting ready to put in your summer bedding. There's a lot of digging out and cleaning to be done. That all takes time. You do a couple of days and then you knock off to do some lawn-mowing and tidying up. There's the edges to be cut and all the normal, everyday jobs. Then you go back to some more of the other work, because this is a really big place and when other jobs crop up you go and do them as well. I was born and bred here and I love it. It's a fine part of the world winter and summer – all the seasons as far as that goes. I do a lot of walking in the

Walter Elsworth has been keeping the gardens at Beaulieu immaculate for over a quarter of a century, to be admired by the many visitors throughout the year.

forest. I like looking for the flowers, the wild flowers out in the woods. I've lived here all my life up to now and, with a bit of luck, I'll live the rest of my life here. I'd be quite happy to do so because I've got that sort of feeling for the place.'

As the rain continues to fall from a leaden sky Walter wheels his barrow into the cloisters, where mediaeval calm still prevails. Not a soul can be seen and the grey stone arches frame the green square of turf in the middle; 'This is the best part of the place. These cloisters are almost timeless. There's little change that I've seen since I was a child. Even the jackdaws are probably related way back. We get a bit of trouble with them because they nest in the holes in the walls. They pick up sticks around the grounds and try to force them in to build their houses. When they won't fit they let them drop on the ground. So, every morning, I have to come along and sweep up the debris. It's a nuisance, but I suppose jackdaws go with the buildings and with the whole atmosphere of the house. Ghosts too, some people think. I've always said I've never seen or heard anything I couldn't understand. I know people in the village, who swear blind that they've heard monks chanting. Some people have spent the night out here just to listen and watch. I have an open mind about it, but I think, in a place like this when you get a moonlit night and the clouds cross the moon, well, with a bit of imagination that can be someone walking. Then perhaps, if you've got a break in one of those leaded windows and the wind gets up, you get a moaning sound or a whistling that isn't very far off music. But some villagers insist that they've seen and heard things no matter what I say.'

The evening closes in early as Walter wheels his barrow slowly back to the shed. Lights shine in the windows of Palace House and reflect it in the puddles on the long paths leading towards it. It has been a cold April day and the traditional showers have lasted for unbroken hours. Only the lovely geese, ducks and ducklings on the Beaulieu river and at Saltmarsh, just to the north of the village, and the gulls, waders and water-birds at Needs Ore on the coast seem to be pleased about the weather.

NEW Forest politics can be turbulent and touchy. Verderers, Commoners, visitors and the Forestry Commission have to try to work together as best they can to maintain what is good in this special part of Hampshire. Often their interests conflict and that can make life difficult for Forestry Commission keepers like Graham Wilson from Kings Hat Cottage, near Beaulieu. But what pleases him most is to be out in the wild, doing his job and enjoying the birds, the animals and the landscapes of the countryside which he loves; 'This forest is about 144 square miles – that's something like 96,000 acres. My responsibility is for about eight to ten thousand of those acres. The job involves protecting my patch from predators, which are harmful to trees or which attack other creatures and, of course, from people too. Vast numbers of visitors come here and we have to control them as gently as possible and to protect the forest as much as we can. Of course, the people who live in the forest and who have lived here over the centuries have done some damage cutting the trees and burning the gorse and so on. But that was acceptable because they were doing it on a small scale. When you're talking about eight to ten million visitors a year, that's another matter entirely. The people that live here twelve months of the year are the ones who are going to be here for the next year and the next and, perhaps, for generations. So they have an interest in preserving where they are living. I think they're fairly responsible. They don't want the place to change and, in my opinion, the older forest people do a lot to keep it good. I suppose you could say too that they're jealous of what they've got. They might have a dig when people encroach on their way of life or onto their territory, and rightly so. They and their ancestors have protected the forest for 900 years and, all of a sudden, there's this emphasis on inviting strangers in and sharing it all with them. Sadly, the old-timers who are the backbone of the place and who have been responsible for its very existence, have been pushed to one side.'

Graham is a big, chunky fellow with a round face and challenging eyes. He does not suffer fools gladly and he is not a man with whom you would choose to tangle. He looks as though he is used to getting his own way. Deer come to graze in the meadow below his cottage. A pony is tethered on the grass on the other side. All around are stacks of wood and the paraphernalia of a man who makes his living off the land; 'My enthusiasm for the forest isn't blunted at all. In fact, it increases. I lead a contented life. I'm sad at having to fit in with modern times and I'm disappointed at some of the changes in the forest. But I'm still here and the place itself makes up for any regrets I may have. I'm in a position where somebody somewhere may still listen and perhaps take advantage of what bit of experience I have. What's more important than that though is that the old foresters – the Verderers and the Commoners – continue to survive and to thrive. The two go hand in glove. One's no good without the other. They are the thin red line that can be traced back through the past nine centuries. There's always been people commoning in the forest and without them we should certainly be lost. Property prices alone could drive them out, so there's a responsibility on the authorities to face up to that problem. Young Commoners, who can be proved to be genuine, should be encouraged and given all possible help to continue their way of life.'

As Graham emphasises, the New Forest would not exist in its present form without the Commoners, whose animals live out on the heathland and graze its lawns. They are the lifeblood of the area and many of their families can be traced back through the centuries. Isaac Keeping from Oldfield Farm, East Boldre, is one of them and his cattle are his career. His son Steve is following in his father's footsteps, offering hope of another generation of the old breed of New Forest Commoners; 'I've been here all my life and I love it. Forest born and bred I am. My view of a Commoner is someone who breeds animals, turns 'em out on the forest and makes his living like that. There's quite a difference between what I do and being a farmer. A farm is a much bigger affair than just a smallholder – and that's what I am really. I've only 15 or 16 acres. But I've got 123 head of cattle, some in buildings but mainly forest cattle, which is what I'm most interested in. Those ones will go as far as Beaulieu Road Station – four or five miles from here. That's when they leave home a little bit later on. They won't want to see me. They won't want to know me all the summer. But when I want them, I know where to go and find them. That's because they run in the same part of the forest every year. They calve in July and I know to a day or two when it's going to happen. A fortnight or three weeks before that time I go and look out those cows that I want and I bring them home, put 'em in the field and keep my eye on them for calving. I don't find any of it much bother because my cows they stay put, in the heart of the forest where there's no roads. And they never get wild at all neither. All I have to do – even when they've been out there for some weeks – is to go and call them and they'll come up to me. Any time of the year. Of course, there are other Commoners' animals out in the general area too. But what is very strange is that my cows run in a particular part, where no others will roam. People have taken theirs up to Beaulieu Road and they won't stay. They wander off. But my cows will stay there and they will stay all the summer. Now I can't answer the question why they like it there. They've always gone up there right from babies and I guess that's where they like to roam.'

Isaac is a thickset man with a red face, thinning grey hair, and kind eyes screwed up against the light. He wears a knitted blue cap, and overalls. Steve, his son, is heavy and dogged. He has inherited his father's determination and his skills. They make a good team as they put the finishing touches to a new barn, which they have built together. Inside are batches of glossy beef animals, which are fed on corn and bedded on straw – very different from the hardy beasts plodding through the forest marshland; 'I'm proud of these ones. And I'm proud of Steve too for designing this building for them. Some of the cattle are ours and some we've bought in. A local farmer helps me find the right ones and, once they're chosen, they'll stay here until they go off to Shaftesbury Market. And they'll go for a good price too. But they needed a special building because they're big creatures and would walk through a lot of ordinary walls. So Steve he drew it all out on paper and we had the Agricultural Advisory Committee down to look at the plans. And they said that what we had done was as good as anything they could have done. The gentleman said that he couldn't teach us anything except perhaps the right mix for the concrete so that it's strong enough for these heavy animals. The best thing is that I feel very lucky to have a son so good that he's interested, and I'm hoping that he's going to follow after me like I did after my father and like he did after his. And for a long time before that too. That makes me feel proud.'

MEMBERS of the Special Operations Executive were trained on Beaulieu Manor Estate during the war, before setting out on their dangerous assignments. A plaque in the cloisters at Palace House, Beaulieu reads; 'Remember before God these men and women of the European Resistance Movement, who were secretly trained at Beaulieu to fight their lonely battle against Hitler's Germany and who, before entering Nazi-occupied Europe, here found some measure of the peace for which they fought.' Today people still come to the New Forest in search of peace and tranquillity from all over the yuppy-occupied south-east of England and from further afield as well. Long may they continue to be able to enjoy such stretches of unblemished countryside as Beaulieu Heath offers, and long may they help to preserve and retain its ancient dignity and stark beauty.

THE TEFFONTS

HIDDEN away off the beaten track, just over the county border, a dozen miles to the west of Salisbury, the two Teffont villages lie in the valley of the tiny river Teff which flows past the doors of the thatched, Chilmark-stone cottages on its way to meet the Nadder a mile to the south-east. The villages were once called Upper and Lower Teffont, but now boast the grander names of Teffont Magna and Evias – said to come from the Welsh word for a ewe. Other than their great beauty and grey dignity, they have few claims to fame – though the first combine harvester to be used in this country was given its baptism on Manor Farm, Teffont Magna in 1934. Today, the little hamlets stand quietly and composed as if hoping that the twentieth century will pass them by, leaving them relatively unscathed. In February, at least, they remain untroubled by noisy invaders and inquisitive trippers.

JOHN Webb has spent his life in the Teffonts, where he was born and bred. He has a Noah's Ark of animals here, including three fine Tamworth pigs, a squadron of cats and some colossal, Christmas turkeys. Just on the edge of the villages he keeps and looks after the loves of his life at the Wessex Shire Park. These sturdy heavy horses are his great pride and he and his team care for them with respect and with much affection; 'I'm very fond of this hidden part of England. South Wiltshire and North Dorset make up one of the most beautiful and spectacular parts of the countryside. Of course, its completely different to the Lake District and the Highlands, but just as good in its own way and very much Thomas Hardy country. Apart from that, it's my roots that keep me here. Once you come to the Teffonts, or to any of the villages in these chalk valleys, it would be a wrench to leave. So you create your own method of staying here. My way has been to introduce Shire horses. It's ironic, because I come from an ancient farming family. They arrived here in 1929 and proceeded to get rid of their Shire horses and to use tractors and combines. Whatever would they say to me now with all these great fellows around me? I dread to think. But it's their fault really because they sat me on one when I was two years old and I've never got over it.'

John is a tall, handsome man with thinning hair and a quick smile. The views from the top of his acres reach to Salisbury Cathedral and beyond. To the west the hill climbs up towards the Dorset border. In the evenings and at dawn, deer cross the hill as they change their feeding-grounds. On his own hillside John stands surrounded by his horses – a dozen in all – some fully grown and some healthy colts. At his call and at the sound of feed buckets the whole bunch of them come lumbering and clumping down the slope snorting with pleasure in anticipation of their evening meal; 'The Shire, I suppose, is the heavy goods vehicle of the horse world. They are renowned as the strongest of the animals. Another cart-horse, the Suffolk Punch, is a very tough beast too in its own right. And it has the benefit that it can stay working for eight hours solid without a rest. But I can't do that and that probably explains why I'm a Shire man. They're not natives of this part of the country. These big Shires have originated in the Midlands. Going back much further though, there have been several strains of Shire horses and they've all come through from the east of England, because that's where the imports of horses have come over the centuries. King John started it all and he named them too. They were brought in from Flanders and landed round the Wash. Then they spread out from there across the country. But the south and the west of England were probably the last areas to get the Shire horse. Many of the older generation of horsemen around these parts still swear by smaller horses – tiny compared to these really big chaps.'

John Webb runs the Wessex Shire Park. These sturdy heavy horses, once a common sight on farms throughout the south, remain a source of pride and affection to devoted country people.

With plaited manes and tails and ribbons in their hair, two massive horses pull a perfectly painted wagon along the old village streets. The clatter of the hooves and the grinding of the metal wheels echo back off the grey stone walls. In the stream trout dart for cover. Overhead, a kestrel keeps a wary eye on the scene; 'I'm afraid I don't think that they'll ever be used widely again on the land. But, if the predictions of some experts and politicians come true, then we're going to see a different set-up of agriculture to what we've got now. They say it will end up with very big farms and with small family farms run as a hobby and not being able to afford high-priced machinery. Those smallholdings will probably benefit by using heavy horses and they'll get enjoyment out of it too. Here in the village, whatever people may think of us, their roses have certainly benefited since we came on the scene. So there are unexpected advantages in keeping Shire horses.'

VIC Goodfellow's home is in Teffont Magna. Every Tuesday he saddles up, climbs on his scooter and heads for Salisbury market to look over the pigs that are being sold and to meet his friends. Vic has spent getting on for a century in the Teffonts and has been a stockman and a gardener. He owns a patch of land on which he has kept his pigs for more than sixty years. Most weeks Vic comes to the local pub – The Black Horse – to collect left-overs to boil up and feed to his hungry charges; 'Do you know, I'm 86 years old, and I've been in the pig trade all me life sorta. 'Cos when I left school and went to work, I had eight sows and a boar to look out for. And you get sort of attached to 'em. Then, of course, when the war come I had to go in the Army, but I still had a couple of pigs home in the sty. 'Twere a job to get any pigs in they days 'cos nobody didn't have any. An old bloke down the road, he said to me that he knowed a bloke that knows another bloke over Langford who had some pigs. He was going over next week to get two of 'em in a wheelbarrow. He went in the middle of the night and pushed the barrow right over to Langford, got his pigs and come back early next morning. That's how keen we was to get hold of 'un.'

Vic has a wheelbarrow too. He steers it carefully out from the back of the village pub. Inside is a gruesome mixture of old bread, lettuce leaves, beer-dregs and left-over meals. You would think that it might rob even a pig of its appetite; 'The secret of success with pigs is not to pay all your money to the miller for food, especially if you're only in a small way of business. If you can pick up some cheap grub and cook it for 'un, that's the answer, because the pig's inside is like human bein's and they like cooked grub. So you gotta treat 'em right, make sure everything's as clean as possible, make sure the potatoes are well boiled and they'll lap it all up. They'll be no trouble and it's the cheapest way too. I've got a hell of a good system going and it's the only way to make anything out of 'un. When I sell the pigs, I don't touch none of that money. Say I clean up between two and three hundred pound. Don't use it; buy some more pigs out of yer pocket-money. That's the whole secret of making it pay. At the same time, make sure they're happy. And the main way to do that is to always come back with more grub. That's all they care. But I can't live without them. No, I can't.'

In Vic's patch a cauldron simmers above a log fire. You would not choose to be down wind of it. The pigs scamper and snuffle round Vic's boots as he sloshes the food into metal troughs. He is a small, bent character with white hair and a curious, lined face which vividly registers all his emotions; 'I was born in Teffont, see. On top of the hill there's a house with a galvanised roof. When you go to Wincanton races or anywhere you'd see it. I was born up there an' I was unwanted sorta. In other words my mother never had a husband. But she was a caretaker, who looked after kids if they had the measles or the mumps or anything. Villagers used to bring 'em up there to her out of the way, so no more'd catch it. I used to spend a lot of time outside The Hole-in-the Wall beer house as a baby to be looked after while my mother was working. And that's how I started drinking. I was in the pram, see, and the lady of the pub – if I kep' making a hell of a big noise – she'd roll up a sugar knob in some muslin and dip'n in cider. And I'd stop howling for half-an-hour. Then, after a bit, she'd dip'n in again. So I had a rosy view of the village. And why not? There isn't any better place. All these woods and hills and that. This village wants a bit of beating. There's plenty'd love to come here. But, unless they got two hundred grand to spend, there's no way they can get in the village. We've still got the poor though as well as the rich. I'm the poor and there's plenty of rich and I don't care what anybody says to the contrary.'

CIS Goodfellow is Vic's daughter-in-law. She is the village postwoman and has been in the Teffonts a mere forty years. Originally from Scotland, she is one of the focal points of the area as she delivers the mail in the morning and, in the afternoon, looks after the tiny Post Office. She is friend, confidante and helper to the people of the villages: 'I've lived in England much longer than I've ever lived in Scotland. This is a lovely place, lovely people and I wouldn't want to live anywhere else now. It's quite a number of things which combine to make it special. It's the villagers, of course, it's very peaceful and the climate is kind – much better than Scotland I can assure you. People say the English village is dying and to a certain extent it may be. But we try to do our best to keep it going. We're in a conservation area and that means building is controlled. And the parish council is careful and they keep their eye on things for us. We have a good spirit too with a garden club and a luncheon club. And, because of my job, I manage to keep in touch with everyone. I quite often do the postal rounds on my bike. The Post Office reckons that I have to ride 11.8 miles a day like that. So it keeps me fit.'

Luckily for Cis, it is a sunny morning as she sets out on her rounds with her satchel bulging with mail. The gardens are thick with daffodils and the tulips are beginning to show. The Teff gurgles and bubbles as it drifts gently beside the street. One of its banks is white with snowdrops. Beneath the surface between the gleaming reflections of the winter sunshine small fish nose their way into the current. The postwoman's

Autumn in Hampshire's New Forest:

> 'I remember, I remember,
> The fir trees dark and high;
> I used to think their slender tops
> Were close against the sky.'   *Thomas Hood*

35

'Yea, the sparrow hath found her an house, and the swallow a nest where she may lay her young.'   Psalm 84

36

Village postmistress Cis Goodfellow rides over ten miles a day around beautiful countryside to deliver the mail to the Teffont villages.

journey takes her to small, uneven cottages and to great stone mansions. She treats all her customers with the same courtesy: 'Not many problems doing this job, though there are a lot of dogs in the village. There are lots more now than there used to be. Some are very nice and some not quite so pleasant. If I'm away and have to have a stand-in, I always warn him about the various different characters. Especially that applies to the houses where it's a bad plan to put your fingers too far into the letter-boxes. On the whole the dogs are fairly well behaved – but not always. Then there's the river. There's no railing or anything so, in a fog, it would be easy to fall in. They say that you're not a true Teffontite until you've been in the river. So I'm still waiting for my baptism. Even when I get it, I still think I'll have a bit of Scotland in my voice. People ask me to do funny things sometimes when I call. It might be to zip up their dress or take the kettle off when it's boiling or perhaps to help them mend something. But the most memorable time was the winter a few years back when I was sliding everywhere and the snow was so deep that I often had to climb through to the doors. Those days I had to go on foot every step of the way to deliver the letters. When I got home I really felt I'd done my day's work and no mistake.'

BY February, pheasant-shooting is over and game-keepers like David Muir are recovering from the non-stop pressure of shooting days. But there is no real respite for them as they prepare for the spring and the breeding season and the return of the guns in October. It's still a long way off, but there's a mass of work to be done during the next six months; 'After we finish shooting at the end of January, we have to turn our attention to catching up the laying birds to produce eggs. That's where the cycle starts. From eggs you get the chicks, which become poults, which in turn become full-grown pheasants. It's the same for us year after year and February is the time for getting the cycle under way. We set up a catcher in the woods. There's food in there and the pheasants go in after it. Once inside they can't escape. Then we go in, catch them up and bring them back to the laying-pens, where we put in something like seven hens to a cock bird. That ratio gives you the right level of fertility. And that's your stock for the season ahead. All these adult birds will be released back into the wild somewhere about the second week in June. After that point the egg production has gone right down low. And you don't want day old chicks being born then anyway because they won't be big or strong enough for the winter months.'

David is a large, brawny man with black hair and an open face. His broad hands are surprisingly gentle as he handles the birds and pushes them into the pens, which stand in rows in a green meadow. Now and again, when he finds one that is not in peak condition, he lets it go. With a clatter of wings it flies back towards the woods, where it was feeding just a few minutes earlier. In the kennels the gun dogs sniff the wind and seem to be wondering why they cannot hear the crack of guns as the pheasants fly; 'The labradors are of all different ages. The very youngest is coming on two and the old lady, as we call her, she's going on fifteen. So she's retired really.

We use them every shooting day for picking up any wounded game and for clearing up behind the guns. They're all more or less related to one another, but what they really have in common is a hell of a lot of training. It's not a case of buying a puppy and then carrying on thinking you've got a trained dog. You put an awful lot of work into it. You only get out of a puppy what you put into it. The instinct to hunt and to retrieve is in most gun dogs. Some dogs hunt more than they retrieve and with some it's the other way round. So my job is to try and bring the two into balance if I can. What you need is for them to hunt and to retrieve at your command, not at their will, which is a big mistake with a lot of dogs. They tend to hunt on their own if they're not controlled. I think the secret in training a dog and making it obedient is in obtaining its trust and its affection. So you must show it friendship and it will trust you in return. All the dogs I've got are in kennels. But there's no reason why you can't have a fully-trained dog that lives in the house with the family. It's just a case of being firm but being kind. You don't need to be overbearing to produce a good gun-dog. It's quite different with pheasants, of course. What makes a strong and healthy bird is the diet you feed it on from the first day it's hatched. Then it's on high protein food and, the older it gets, the more you drop the level of the protein until you reach a time when they're old enough to eat just corn on its own. It's not as easy as it may sound but, if you achieve it, that produces strong and healthy pheasants.'

Deep in the farmland and a mile from the nearest road the big man strides down a muddy lane with his dogs clustering round his feet and constantly looking upwards for signs of approval. It's a raw February day but there's work to be done and they are all too occupied to notice the weather; 'I think Teffont is a super place. It nestles in the chalk downland and it's this sort of country at its very best. The flowers and animals in this area are fantastic. I don't think a lot of people appreciate that because they don't get out to see it. I live with it seven days a week and I suppose I can enjoy it more than most. It's part and parcel of my job to live with and to absorb everything that moves and lives round here.'

THE buildings at Manor Farm, Teffont Magna, where Peter Brougham carries on his demanding work as a wheelwright, have been used by the villagers for parties saluting the Jubilee and the Coronation – and probably for other, more distant celebrations too. Today they offer shelter to Peter as he caters for those who still love to drive horses and carriages on traditional old-fashioned wheels; 'I started doing all this as a hobby. I owned a pub at the time and I bought a cart. I wanted to know how to do it up, so I went and found a wheelwright where I lived. I asked him plenty of stupid questions. I suppose, like a lot of people, when you want to learn something, it's a matter of watching and remembering and then asking silly questions. They're idiotic to the people who know something about the craft but they weren't to me at the time. Over a period of fifteen years now I've learnt by experience and I built up the business to a point where I could go full-time wheelwrighting, and earn a living at it. I'll never make a fortune because people don't seem to want to pay much for skills that are done by hand. But you'll always earn enough and it's a pleasant thing to do. To make ends meet we sometimes have to do other things too so that the pennies come together. There's a lot of real satisfaction in working with your hands and producing something which you've taken from start to finish, instead of just a little part of it. It becomes even more satisfying when you can invent ways as you go along of doing things better. Because, with many of these old crafts, there is a lot of what you might call black art – rule of thumb in other words. The old-timers would say that this was the way it had always been done, but they couldn't really tell you how to go about it. It was just the habit of a lifetime. So you had to work out for yourself a hell of a lot of minute details as to how things went together or why they were done. Today we use as much machinery as the job allows us to, because time is the biggest element of cost in any job. So now we use new machines to do old jobs.'

The workshop is in the old farm granary where the two hundredweight hemp sacks of corn were once stored. It is at the top of some narrow wooden steps leading up from the yard below. Many a bent back must have groaned under the weight of those heavy bags in decades past. Now there is a different scene with spokes, hubs, saws, lathes and finished wheels jostling for position. In the midst of it all, Peter works slowly and methodically doing the impossible for any but the most skilled; 'A lot of the time jobs are done better with machinery because it's more accurate. You can set machines to be infinitely precise whereas, if you do it by hand, you are going to have a discrepancy somewhere. At the end of the day, though, even when using machines, you have to finish a lot of the jobs off by hand because, perhaps encouragingly, there's still some jobs which the machine can't do. Spokes are a perfect example of where the machine comes into its own. Years ago it was all done with a draw-knife, a spoke-shave and a plane. Today we can put them on a moulding machine with a cutter and, with two passes through the slot, we've got a finished spoke. And every one is identical to the last. Olden days there was a little bit of deviation, although ordinary people didn't realise it. Even in the 1920s though, there was some machinery being used for this job and there were firms supplying manufacturing wheelwrights with identical spokes all those years ago. Doing it today, it's a question of having an aptitude for it. If you like wood-working and if you enjoy doing things with your hands and you are at one with your material, then it becomes easy. You need to learn to take it step by step and to break it down into small stages. You need to learn each stage and the reason why you do it and then it becomes quite simple. It's like what they say – when you know how, it's easy.'

In a nearby field a group of schoolchildren sits on a pile of weathering logs watching as Peter, helped by David Muir, the game-keeper, stokes a burning circle of flaming wood. The children enjoy the spectacle as well as the warmth on a grey winter's afternoon. At their village houses, homework awaits them, so there is every incentive to stay put; 'What we've got to do is to heat the bond that's in the bonfire until it's very hot indeed. The bond is the metal ring that goes round the outside of the wheel. When it's red-hot we'll take it out with tongs and, because it will have

40

expanded in the heat, it will be bigger than the wheel. When it was cold it was half an inch smaller than the circumference of the wheel. So we'll drop it over the wheel and quench it with water. That will shrink it round the wheel and pull it up tight. And you'd be surprised what an enormous amount of power there is as that metal contracts and builds the wheel firmly in.'

As the daylight fades, the falling water splutters and roars as it meets the red steel. The metal bites into the wood and holds it tight. The fire begins to die and slowly, reluctantly, the children head home across the fields. In the distance the village looks warm and prosperous as the lights come on and the chimneys begin to smoke.

TISBURY lies three miles to the west of the Teffonts. Here, Reg Sanger, who lives in Ebenezer Cottage and is 78 years old, is a dab hand at pickling. He has been doing this difficult work to his own recipes for more than thirty years, and his eggs, onions and red cabbage are enjoyed in twenty local pubs, including the Black Horse at Teffont Magna; 'When I first started I wasn't doing a big range. What really got me going was when I lost me leg. That was eight years ago and I couldn't get about. I thought pickling was the best thing I could do to occupy my mind. So I've gone from there and, as well as onions, I picked up eggs and red cabbage. I thought of the cabbage, because one day I was sitting in a cafe and I saw this man eating pickled cabbage and it was hanging down from his mouth, long streaks of it. And I thought to meself, I'm sure I could do better than that. So I chopped it up fine. That went well for a time. But, after a while, I found I could improve it by adding sugar. When I'm talking of sugar I must explain that it's got to be Whitworths brown sugar. I've tried all sorts of cheap sugar, but it don't dissolve in the vinegar. So it must be Whitworths and I use the best vinegar, Sarsons brown malt vinegar, 'cos it's already been boiled. My pickles is wonderful because they haven't got the tartness of the onion or of the vinegar. I mean, to drink vinegar it's terrible and that little bit of sugar just takes what we call the twang off. Women go crazy for 'em.'

As he sits in his wheelchair, Reg carefully cuts vegetables, peels eggs and onions and adds delicate quantities of sugar, salt and vinegar. Around him stand dozens of jars full of his painstaking work. The colours – browns, purples, whites and greens – make a delicate tapestry on the shelf behind him; 'The only thing with pickling eggs is that they must be ten days old before you boil 'em. You boil 'em in cold water. When they come to the boil you let 'em bubble for five to six minutes. Then you switch off the heat. But then you must leave 'em on the ring for at least another five minutes. So you can say about a quarter of an hour simmering and boiling. Next you tip 'em into a bowl of cold water. You crack each egg, put it back into the cold water so it allows the shell to remove and then the shell comes off – but the skin have also gotta come off with the shell. That's the most important thing with a pickled egg. With onions it's quite simple. Again, I use Sarsons vinegar, and I put salt with every drop of vinegar I use. So they're already salted. Apart from that I put Whitworths sugar with 'em – like with the cabbage – and that's what makes 'em so pleasant and eatable. I would say at a darts match they can use anything up to half a gallon of my onions. They're very, very popular and if you were to eat an onion that were not my onion and then eat my onion you'd definitely know the difference. A vast difference. In spite of me leg I still go out every day. Each morning from eleven to three pub drinking. If I sell a jar of onions then I have an extra drop. I never go just to one pub. I go to four or five pubs a day.'

THE two Teffont villages stand, in the main, as they have stood for centuries, the old stone weathered and wind-beaten and unchanging in all the seasons of the year. Newcomers have arrived and house prices have soared. But some of the old character and, more important, the old-timers, have remained and are as unchanging as the cottages they live in. An old ditty, sung in distant days by the village sports teams, is as charming as the place itself:

> 'T.E.F.F.O.N.T.
> You may beat eggs
> But you can't beat we.
> There's trout in the river
> And snakes in the grass
> In Teffont Magna and Evias.'

THE MELBURYS

THE three Melbury villages lie close to the south of Sherborne in the county of Dorset and encompass much that is best in that matchless part of England. In a year when spring came early, the local people, who know about these things, said that Nature was four or five weeks ahead of herself. Thomas Hardy's mother once had her home in Melbury Osmond and the streets are full of those hidden corners and secret places dear to her son's heart. In *The Woodlanders* Hardy describes the village as 'one of those sequestered spots outside the gates of the world where may usually be found more meditation than action and more listlessness than meditation; where reasoning proceeds on narrow premises and results in inferences wildly imaginative . . . .' Melbury Bubb, named after the Saxon, Bubba, who lived there, and Melbury Sampford make up the trio of enchanted hamlets.

DAWN Warr lives with her parents and plenty of dogs in Valley Cottage, Melbury Sampford. It is a Hansel and Gretel house with a long thatched roof, a tiny stream rippling through the garden and stands of mighty trees surrounding it on every side. Dawn is a fine shot and a talented naturalist. She earns her living as a gamekeeper – an unusual job for a young woman even in these liberated days. Recently she has been making a name for herelf by the skill with which she stuffs and mounts dead birds and animals; 'This is part of old England here. The trees, the isolation, the atmosphere – you couldn't ask for better really. It's a tied cottage. In gamekeeping that's always the case. But they're not all as pretty as this one, though they're nearly always on their own with no neighbours. I've been gamekeeping now for nearly thirteen years. When I started there wasn't very much female keepers about. But these days there seem to be a few more of them. My Dad had been a gamekeeper ever since I can remember and my elder brother's one too. So it sort of came naturally. I've always been out with Dad and it's what I've wanted to do. This is the best way you can do a job in the countryside. You have to be tough and you build up a lot of muscles. You've got to do a lot of lifting, a lot of hard physical work and long hours. But you are your own boss to a degree and you've got fascinating work.'

The feeding pens are on a hillside close by the cottage. From her home Dawn would hear any disturbance caused by visiting foxes. In the early dawn she walks slowly out to where the swiftly growing young pheasants prowl round the perimeter wire. Whistling softly to them and making no sudden movements, she spreads corn in steady streams onto the ground. A bold cock pheasant, his haughty black, red and blue head held high, stalks fearlessly behind her helping himself to the best grains. In his train follow a timid group of hen pheasants, less exotic but just as lovely in their own quieter way; 'They started laying yesterday. Just a couple of eggs we get to start with. It will build up until we're getting about 150 to 180 a day. So we've got a way to go yet. This winter has been so mild. Everything seems to be forward. The leaves are starting and the bluebells is up, the little birds is laying. And so, although it's a bit early yet, the pheasants will be ahead of themselves too, I should think. But we're not only rearing pheasants. We've also got to look after the rest of the wildlife. We don't just go round shooting everything, you know. There's a balance in Nature and you try and keep it. And you have to work at that all the time. You get up early each morning. In the summer I'm up before six. I don't finish until ten or eleven at night. That's a long day and it's seven days a week March until Christmas. I don't get a lie-in at all until Christmas Day. Then I feed the pheasants the night before just on dark, so that their food is ready and waiting for them next morning, but still I wake up the normal time even so. I'm also working in all weathers out in the woods and you don't have much to do with people. I don't like people a lot. I like to be out on my own working with animals. And they get to know you. When you're feeding the pheasants in the winter you have lots of finches and blackbirds and other birds come on the feedline. In a hard time you're saving their lives 'cos they get their share of the corn. You're feeding the ducks in the frost and snow too. When it's all frozen up you keep them going. And all these birds get used to you walking around. You feed the pheasants the same time of day as the sun rises. So you're a part of Nature to them and they don't take any notice of you.'

Dawn has brown curly hair and a fresh, attractive face. She is a strong character and pleasantly outspoken. In a shed above Valley Cottage are birds and animals, which she has stuffed. They look glossy and handsome as she combs and smooths out their fur and feathers; 'I enjoy doing this because you start with a dead body and then, with your skill, you change it into something that looks living. You get a kick out of it when people tell you they look real and alive. It started when I was on holiday with my gamekeeper brother in Shropshire. He had a few stuffed animals about – a mink and a stoat, I think. And I thought that I'd like to try and preserve the predators like mink that I catched in tunnel traps. Soon after, a man brought in an owl that had been knocked down and killed and asked me if I would do that. And it's built up from there. Now I do a lot of things for people whenever I can, but I don't get that much time. One thing I wouldn't ever stuff is somebody's pet. I've been asked to several times. Once a man rang me up and said would I stuff his labrador, and I thought he was pulling me leg. I said "Why do you want him stuffed? Is he noisy?" And he said, "No, he's in the freezer". The reason I won't do a pet is that, with a wild animal, you only have to work to get it looking natural. But with a pet you have to get its character and that's nearly impossible.'

Half a mile from the cottage lies a large, calm lake with a thatched boat-house at one end, jetties for fishermen round the margin and swans, ducks, coots and moorhens enjoying the hospitality of the water. Reeds surround the lake and perfect reflections of mature trees lie untroubled on its surface. Here Dawn brings her dogs for exercise and training. They wait, transported, on the edge and, at her word of command, all five plunge in like Olympic racers in pursuit of the stick, which their mistress has thrown; 'We've got two big Alsatians for security and against poachers and then we've got the working dogs. That's three golden retrievers and two springer spaniels. It's great for them out in the lake. They love it and it gives them a relaxing time swimming about. We train them all ourselves. With the Alsatians, if you get into difficulty and you are attacked, they will protect you. 'Cos with modern day poaching it can be quite nasty. The dogs can only defend you if you are attacked. You can't just let them go up and bite anybody. You would be against the law then. But if you are out late at night – and in the winter one of us is out every night on poacher duty – it gives you a bit more confidence to have one of them with you. The working dogs aren't too difficult to train. You want to get them from a working home. The younger the puppy the better I always find. Like you get them seven and a half to eight weeks old and then you can bring them on as you want to. Some people start training them too early I always think. It's like with kids. You want to let them play around and have a bit of fun first. So, up until about six months old, they just run about with the rest of the dogs. But in that time they learn to sit when the others sit and come to the whistle and know their name. So that's their basic training. Then, with these gun dogs, retrieving seems to be a natural instinct in them. If they've got a piece of wood you just encourage them to bring it to you. Even if they've got something smelly like a bit of cow-dung, it's no good chasing them and saying, "Put that down". You must always encourage them to bring it to you and say, "What a lovely dog. Isn't that good? How kind of you to bring it to me." It takes two years to get a puppy trained. So, when your best dogs are seven or eight, that's the time to get another puppy to replace them, so that in a couple of years he'll be there to take over. You have to think ahead all the time like that. But you couldn't do your job at all easily without the dogs – they're like a tractor to a farmer.'

As Dawn walks softly down a long gravel track in the woods, the mist begins to clear from the surrounding Dorset hills. In the valley below a group of timid fallow deer graze, look up alertly and graze again. Deep amongst the trees a cock pheasant gives his heavy bark.

BUBB Down Farm is one of the six houses which make up the village of Melbury Bubb. Mrs Dollery may have been describing the hamlet in *The Woodlanders* when she said, ''Tis such a little place that you'd need have a candle and lantern to find it'. John Broadway is the farmer and his 85 cows keep him and his son busy all the year round; 'It's quiet here all right. But 'tis what you get used to. We've always enjoyed living here. I have anyways. It's where I was born and, bar two years when I moved a couple of miles away, I've lived here all the time. So I should know it quite well after fifty seasons or so. It's good enough all year round. Autumn might be best because all the work's done then and you feel you can relax a bit. But then there's the spring, which is the beginning of everything. You've got to look forward to all the

John Broadway farms in the tiny hamlet of Melbury Bubb where he has lived all his life.

haymaking, the silage-making and all the work coming on. But 'tis both a nice time really. We used to stand and look at the hills and views more than we do now. Take 'un a bit for granted these days you know. We used to walk up on the hills too when we were younger. The only thing you walk after now is the cattle when they get out. But life was steadier them days, you see. Even out here we're in the sort of mad rat race. Them times 'twas sort of 35 cows. Now we got 85. Old times there's more people on the farm to do the work. Now we've only got the wife, son, daughter-in-law. That's all and nearly three times as many to milk.'

The voice is full of Dorset. There is sadness in the face but humour as well. Wind, rain and frost have taken their toll. But this is a man who will not be rushed or hurried. He is stubborn and reliable; 'We didn't sorta see nobody too much them days. We were a bit shy I s'pose. No cars or anything. Used to walk two miles there and two miles back to school every day. We've always been a village on our own and always will be I think.'

When John can find the time, he likes to slip over the hill to the Strangways Arms at Holywell to play skittles with his friends. The alley is old and venerable. The balls rattle and roar on their way down to the pins which they hit and scatter with venomous impact. The beer flows and the conversation is of cattle and sheep, grass and corn. The faces are red and healthy, the arms strong and thick, the atmosphere loud and friendly; 'We have a game a week all through the winter. Tonight is a friendly between Melbury Bubb and Melbury Osmond. Most of 'em here is farmers of one kind or another. We'll have a good night of it for sure. We like to win, but we don't mind too much if we lose. After you've had a hard day, especially in the winter, 'tis a good relaxation. Skittles is a game which anybody can play. You mightn't have tried it at all before and you can come along and beat someone who's always playing. That's the beauty of the game. 'Tis a real leveller. And it's simple too. There's nine pins and you have three balls. The alley's probably ten, fifteen yards long. The skittles is in a sorta diamond shape and you gotta try and knock 'em all down. If you roll the first ball and they all go down, that's what they call a flopper. If you get 'em all with two, that's a spare. Because then you gotta spare ball look, and they put all nine up again so you have another go with your odd ball. So you could, if you was very lucky, get as many as 27 if you had a flopper with each of your three balls. Right at the end of the evening we have a beer hand and, whichever team loses it, pays for the evening's drinking. So we all try quite hard then.'

Outside in the night, the sounds from the pub are cheerful and warming. A tawny owl flies softly overhead on its deadly rounds. In the far distance a fox screams at the narrow new moon.

MEAD Cottage in Melbury Osmond is thatched and squat and homely. It is next door to the house where Thomas Hardy's mother grew up. This is the house of Esmie Flatman – a sprightly 76 year old school-teacher, organist and backbone of the village; 'I came here 36 years ago and there's something very special about it all.

47

What it is I'm not sure but I've never found anywhere else with so much friendliness. It's pretty of course. But it's not just that. Nothing ever hurries here. If you come home from somewhere where you've had a pretty hectic time, it's always relaxing to be back. When you come over the hills from Shaftesbury you can feel you're in Dorset straight away. Most people probably feel good about getting to their homes, but this place is unique I think.'

Esmie's garden is stacked up steeply at the side of her cottage in small steps full of flowers and shrubs. She spends much of her time working in it and keeping it fresh and colourful; 'It's a perfect, sunny spot – facing south, you see. The garden itself wasn't very pretty when I came here. I've worked really hard to get it right. That's a good thing too, because if you go to a place and the garden is ready and you don't like it, maybe you'll have to accept it as it is. Whereas, if you inherit a rough, old thing that's not any good, you can turn it into what you like. Round about here nothing much has changed since I first came. It's all estate property and it's farmland. So we stay just as we are. We're lucky people.'

With her gardening, Esmie is never short of exercise. But she gets plenty of extra walking when she climbs to the top of the steep hill on which her cottage stands. On it stands the church in which Thomas Hardy's mother was baptised and married and where Esmie regularly provides the music; 'It must have been over thirty years ago now when the last organist gave up. Well, the rector came down one day and asked me if I'd fill in for a while until they could find someone else. I wasn't all that keen but I filled in. And I'm still filling in. It's a lovely old organ and it used to be hand-pumped. There was a terrible handle that went up and down. A mixture of people used to volunteer to do it. Some did it with a great thump. Some dozed off. Some did it too slowly and then the organ used to gasp in the middle of the music. I'd be playing away with all the stops out and the sound would get fainter and fainter. We didn't have electricity in Melbury Osmond for a long time. But when it eventually came, the organ was electrified and now it's much better, though I haven't any excuse if I don't play well. The other great pleasure for me is when my old pupils come back to see me – the ones I've taught and are now living sometimes far away with families of their own. They come back to talk and to reminisce. All the naughty little boys have turned into well-mannered men. The years have tamed them in some way.'

The sound of the organ drifts across the meadows. A squirrel is hard at work in a nearby beech tree. In the rookery across the valley the great, black birds add their voices to the accompanying music.

IT is a surprise to find a thriving vet's practice in as small a village as Melbury Osmond. But the local farmers are pleased that it is there and close at hand. Bob Oaksford is one of the three partners and he has covered most of the narrow lanes and the farms in the area many times over; 'It's not a job to pretend about this. It's long hours and it can be hard work. It can be wet and it can be cold. But it's not so bad. If you've got a reasonable practice, you can share the workload with others and have a break every now and then. This season's been about average round these parts. Lambing has been about normal I should say. Animal health has been good during the winter because it's been dry and not too cold. There's no such thing as the regular farm for a vet. It's all very variable. Seasonal too. A sheep farm in the lambing season I might visit quite often and the rest of the year hardly at all. But it would be a different pattern with other types of enterprise. With dairy farmers, for instance, most of the work is in the autumn and very little in the summer. Cats and dogs and that sort of thing seem to come in the hot months. So it spreads itself through the year.'

Up on the downs Bob stands beside the solid figure of farmer, Geoff Stenhouse, watching as Andrew Stenhouse catches a lame ewe and sets her comfortably on her rump. The sun shines on the grass and the rest of the flock scatters in alarm; 'Mostly at this time of year we're dealing with lambing problems. It's the young lambs which sometimes get into difficulties. And, of course, there's always foot trouble with sheep and that's a year round thing. It really keeps the shepherd busy more than us though. Geoff and Andrew have done very well this year. They've had very few hardships and everything seems to have gone smoothly. They're nearly at the end of lambing now so all should be well, particularly with this nice weather. As for me, my schedule is as uncertain as it always is. This job is like that. We don't know from one day to the next what we're going to be doing. But I hope that there are not too many more sleepless nights ahead now. However tired you are though, it's a good time to be out and about. You notice more rapid change at this time of year than at any other. There's a new colour in the greenness of the hedges every day as you go by. The blackthorn is coming out and everything is changing. The lambs grow so fast you don't believe it and, with a fine day like this, spring is definitely on the way. In fact, the only problem is these narrow lanes when you're driving. But you get used to them too in the end. Most of the people coming the other way are used to them too, thank goodness. So we manage to hit one another only now and again.'

MELBURY Bubb Cottage is home to Sue Waterman and her race-horses. She is a National Hunt and Point-to-Point jockey and has all the modest courage which the job demands. Her day begins early with preparing and training her horses for the tough races which lie ahead; 'It's not only a beauty spot. It's a good place for horses too. Because it's so quiet. You get a lot of young horses that don't like traffic very much and you can introduce them slowly. All they'll see is a few tractors in these parts. I've just got two of my own at the moment. I've loved horses all my life ever since I was a baby and, once you get involved with them, you just can't give them up. We can ride all up around here in the woods and on the lanes. We cover about ten miles a day when we're exercising. And everywhere within a radius of five miles, whichever direction you go, you can always see Melbury Bubb.

The early sunshine cuts hard shadows on the stable-yard as Sue saddles up. The

National Hunt jockey Sue Waterman trains racehorses at Melbury Bubb.

horses are fired up and ready for action. Dogs and cats look on disdainfully at the bustle and the activity. Sue's strong hands adjust straps, tug at buckles, pick up hooves and push in bits as the horses stamp and snort in anticipation of adventures ahead. She is a tall, wiry woman with a quick smile, a tanned face and challenging eyes; 'They're racing machines really. My permit allows me to train my own for National Hunt – hurdling, steeple chasing and that kind of thing. It's grand to have a really good one and that sometimes happens. But, in between, you get loads that aren't so hot and they're sold on as hunters or show-jumpers. Both these ones have shown some ability this year, so they'll be staying on for a while. I've won four races now and I'm pleased enough about that. But it's difficult winning nowadays. You've got loads of Arabs involved and they buy the best. So you've got to have a really good horse. The standards are getting higher all the time. People say it's dangerous and I suppose it can be. But you don't think about that when you're racing. All you do is concentrate on riding your very best. The ones who get excited are the horses. They know something's up when you start to get them ready on race mornings. You only have to go and get out a travelling rug and some bandages or start plaiting their manes and they're shaking all over. They know straight away when they're going racing. The thing about it is that a racehorse has always got to be 110% fit. That's because it's got to find that little bit more right at the end of the race if it's going to do well. And the hills and steep banks round here are just the job for that. We'll work them up to the top and do some steady cantering. Probably we'd go up three times in a day, which makes them puff and blow. But it gets them fit and muscles them up tremendously, especially on the back-end. So they're a godsend these hills really.'

THERE are sixteen packs of mink hounds in the country and one of them is cared for and run by Rosie Whitcomb at Clift Lane, Toller Porcorum – just to the south of the Melburys. Sometimes Rosie takes the hounds to the banks of the river Frome in Maiden Newton for exercise and refreshment in its cooling waters; 'I've worked in kennels for forty years now. I moved down to Cattistock, where I thought I might retire because it was such a good place. And I was getting fed up with working such long hours. Then I heard of this kennels up at Toller and here I am. I've been scrapping around with hounds for donkey's years. I just can't keep my sticky fingers out. I've got fifteen couple of hounds here. There's two lines. There's the pure-bred otter-hound. And there's the cross-bred – sorta otter, fox and bloodhound combined. I must admit that they're my favourites. But I've got four generations of the pure-bred now. Unlike the foxhounds they're slow to grow up. Oozle, whose done three full seasons, still behaves like a puppy. She's very low-scented. Her great-grandad was the lowest scenting hound we ever had. Old Linguist he was called. He could pick up a mink three miles before you found it. If he didn't open his gob you could be absolutely sure there was nothing on the water. He had a lovely voice, and his daughter too. And he was a brave dog. One of his offspring will jump off a twenty foot bank and not even turn his head – and he got that from Old Linguist. And when they were hollering and bawling and yawping away you could always hear him above the rest.'

It is a memorable sight as Rosie leads her pack into the water. Some of the great, shaggy animals jump in with a mighty splash. Others tread more gingerly. Rosie herself marches in up to the waist of her corduroy trousers untroubled by cold or wet and her voice vying with the best of them; 'We hunt regular on Saturdays. And we do one evening – sometimes two – during the week. When we get to September and there's a lot of water in the river we sometimes have to go back up the stream and do it again. That's 'cos we've missed one that we knew was there. You see, we don't take no prisoners, not where mink's concerned. We reckon to catch 'em and, if we leave one behind because we can't get it or we lose it, we'll go back. You see, mink are vicious. They kill anything. Mink will try to kill dogs. Get hold of a terrier and pull it into the water. One of our blokes had to dive in once 'cos a mink took his dog under and he had to pull it back up. The reason I don't wear wellies for this job is because they're not safe. Wellies fill with water and you get dragged under by the weight. Boots are better. They're firmer for walking on the stony banks too. You get wet, of course. But that's part and parcel of the job. The old otter-hunters used to have holes put in their insteps so's the water drained out. But, by the time you've worn boots on this job for six months they've got holes in them anyway. 'Cos the water rots the stiches.'

As the pack of hounds follow Rosie down the bank to the meadows beyond the nearby trees, ducks float complacently on the water apparently unafraid of the commotion or of the strong, snapping jaws.

THERE is a signpost at the bottom of the lane which leads to Melbury Bubb. The circle at the top is marked 'Hell Corner'. What faraway tragedy gave birth to such a description? For here, in fact, is a small corner of heaven. In *The Woodlanders* Thomas Hardy wrote that this countryside 'cannot be regarded as inferior to any inland scenery of the sort in the West of England or perhaps anywhere in the Kingdom'. There is a grandeur about this part of Dorset which can only be described by great wordsmiths. It is as though Nature had tried to achieve perfection here and, in spite of man's best endeavours to the contrary, had come close to succeeding.

Foxgloves add their wild beauty to summer woodlands and heaths. They can grow anywhere in safety since even the hungriest animals leave their lush-looking leaves alone in all seasons. They produce a poisonous drug called digitalis and taste foul.

53

Toadstools are the most persecuted of plants. People trample and destroy them because they believe – sometimes correctly – that they are poisonous. But they have a beauty and a colour and a texture equalled by few other wild things.

WEYHILL

THE village of Weyhill stands on the high ground to the west of Andover in the county of Hampshire. Until quite recent times this pretty village was famous for its week-long fair. It was, as they say in the country, 'a big 'un'. It had everything – horses, sheep, cattle, produce, hops, as well as entertainment and a great deal of beer. In *The Mayor of Casterbridge* Thomas Hardy had Henchard sell his wife at Weyhill Fair after he had had a skinful. In his *Hampshire Village Book*, Anthony Brode wrote that in 1876 'a newspaper reported that "trade generally was very dull." At what was still "the largest fair in England", the number of sheep sold that October was between "12,000 and 15,000 below the average. The so-called pleasure fair was at its zenith and, in spite of mud and filth ankle deep, the stalls were well attended".' Mr Brode also says that, traditionally, this was the fair Johnny was so long at. If so, it is not hard to guess the reason why. Back into history, such autumn festivities were renowned for their carousing and womanising. Poor Johnny must have eventually reached home rather the worse for wear.

TODAY thousands flock to Weyhill again through the spring, summer and autumn months. But now it is for an entirely different reason. Gone are the tents and the rings of the great jamboree. In their place stand airy cages full of great and beautiful birds. In the middle is a spacious grass arena where they fly and show off their extraordinary skills. For this is the home of The Hawk Conservancy, which is run by Reg Smith, his son Ashley and their friend Jim Chick, who is Director of the British Falconers Club. Reg Smith is short, blunt and gnarled. His eyes shine with youthful enthusiasm in spite of his years. He is a supreme communicator and particularly about his passion for birds; 'We started the Hawk Conservancy here at Weyhill about 23 years ago. It came about because of my deep love of the countryside. For me a bird of prey is the symbol of the country. Its wildness, its beauty and the untamed quality, which all birds of prey possess, is what makes me appreciate them. It's also the total independence of the bird. In no way is it subservient to me in any single regard. It's not a pet bird. It never will be. We work as equal partners. In fact, sometimes it's not equal. She's in charge of me. It's a privilege to work with a creature in that way. When you compare it to the raucous behaviour and the bright colours of a parrot, for instance, it's no contest. This is pure beauty in bird form. When they are flying, it's poetry in the air. Their appreciation of winds, thermal conditions and air currents is magical. I suppose the nearest thing you get to it in human form is the yachtsman or perhaps the captain of an old clipper ship. The best of them have a knowledge of weather conditions that enables them to move under any circumstances. Our birds here are not tame. There is no such thing as a tame bird of prey. It's a job to explain the relationship until you've been working with them for a few years. The bird is totally independent when it is in flight. The only control you have is the training that you've put into it. There's certainly no question of them obeying you. The secret is that they need you as much as you need them. It's a true partnership.'

There are 57 different species of birds of prey at Weyhill. They are divided up into hawks, falcons, eagles, vultures and owls. One of the questions, which is always asked by visitors, is what happens to the birds in the winter. The surprising reply is that nothing happens in the winter. All the problems are in the summer. All the mews – the hawks' cages – and the weathering grounds are in the shade. Heat is the enemy of the bird of prey.

While Reg is on his rounds looking individually at each of his precious charges, checking, noting, cleaning and feeding, Ashley and Jim Chick are on their way to nearby East Cholderton, where a farmer is keen to restore barn owls to his buildings. There are two fine, young owls in a box in the back of the car, and Jim and Ashley have already fixed a tea-chest in the roof of the old building as a home for them. The farmer, an old man with white hair and a quick smile, meets them when they arrive. His black labrador waddles behind him, slumps down on the ground and greedily eyes the two birds with their smooth white and beige feathers. The farmer is delighted to see them; 'We used to have them in the barn for years and years. They'd run along under the eaves and, in our bedroom, you could hear their pattering at nights, going out and coming back in. But they've been gone for a long time now, for what reason I don't know. All birds are beautiful to me. This year we're short of swallows and house-martins. Always in the past we've had them building their mud nests up under the eaves. I think it's because we've got a lot of magpies. They're vicious birds and have chased them away.' The old face saddens but then lights up again; 'We'll be pleased to have the owls again. They're so pretty.'

Inside the barn with its mighty beams and arching roof, Jim Chick climbs a tall ladder towards where the tea-chest is firmly secured. Ashley watches anxiously from below and, while the farmer holds one of the birds, he mounts the ladder behind Jim and gently hands him an owl; 'We've got a lot of them at the Hawk Conservancy. We get injured ones brought in with broken legs or wings. They can't be released back into the wild, so we run a breed and release scheme with them. All of the young that we manage to breed are set free. That's what we're doing with Mr Knight here. He has a lovely farm with all the hedgerows left in, beautiful old buildings and a perfect situation for barn owls. So we're letting him have a young pair in his barn. Let's hope they'll stay. We'll have to keep the barn doors shut for about eight weeks. During that time the owls will live inside the barn and get used to their new home. Then we open the doors and they have the opportunity of staying put or of moving on to another site. And some die. You have to be realistic about that. You never get a 100% success rate. Some don't make it that are born out in the wild. Probably as many as 70% of birds in the wild, and especially more vulnerable ones like barn

Ashley Smith holds two barn owl chicks. It is difficult to believe that these fluffy creatures will grow into perfect hunting machines.

owls, will die or be killed. One of the reasons for that is the change in farming techniques. The combine harvesters arrived round here in about 1940, so we didn't have any ricks after that. Around the farmyards, there were no easy areas for mice and voles to live and nothing much for them to eat either. And that meant a lot less for the barn owl to hunt. Of course, another factor is that there are a lot of tawny owls round here now. The two aren't compatible. Tawnys will actually drive barn owls away. But not these ones. We all hope that they'll stay here for many years to come.'

Back at Weyhill Reg Smith is preparing to run a display for a group of fifty schoolchildren. They are happy and excited as they sit on wooden benches in the warm, September sunshine. Reg watches them from the wings; 'I was brought up with birds of prey as a small boy. For me, they are my life. After a while you start to think like one. And you look for characteristics in people that you find in hawks or falcons. Their elegance in flight is probably as fantastic as anything you'll ever see. It's breath-taking and rewarding beyond anything I can describe. You can see it on the kids faces as they watch. One reason for the success we have, I believe, is that this place is for the birds rather than for the people.'

Reg walks to a battered stool facing the audience and settles on it. He is roughly dressed and outspoken with the children. There is absolute silence, broken by gasps of amazement, as they watch and listen; 'We're going to be flying these birds on both sides of you, children, over the back and in the front here. So, once we've got them in the air, keep to your seats and don't move about. The first one is Clara. She's an African Fish Eagle. She's about 27 years old, but she's only been flying here for the past six months. In Africa she's very famous for her voice and the great cawing noise she makes. Her Latin name means 'Salt Water Eagle whose voice carries' and, in those countries, the sound is called 'The Voice of Africa'. Look at her strength in flight. All the power is in the early part when the bird is using its engine, the pectoral muscles in its chest, and that initial thrust is followed by a glide, which will take her right over your heads. Her lovely black, white and brown colouring comes in the third year of her life. They're very long-lived eagles these, and they sometimes carry on for as much as seventy years. None of this sort are being bred in Britain at the moment, though there are some in Germany I think. It's important to keep them going because nearly all African animals and birds are in danger. When you've got a country that has a terrible starvation problem, then the conservation of birds and animals takes a very low priority. You've got to provide food for people. So it's important for fortunate countries like ours to try and propagate birds like Clara, because one day we might have to start thinking about taking them back to Africa and letting them go free.'

One thing in short supply during Reg's demonstration is boredom. There is no pretence in the children's eagerness as they watch the great birds wheel, swoop, dive and land. All the time Reg feeds information and facts into the young heads. It is a high-class educational experience for them. The last bird is the star of the show; 'This is a British bird of prey and it's the commonest of nocturnal birds. It's a tawny owl and his name is Chestnut. This is the owl that lives in the woods – the one that goes twit-twoo in the night. Chestnut is only a youngster so he can't do that yet. He just makes a mixture of a squeak and a whistle, which means 'hallo'. These aren't endangered at all. In fact, they've increased in the last years. They even go into the towns. I was in London the other month and we went through St James's Park and there were two tawny owls sitting right at the top of one of those big trees. If any of you ever find an injured bird of prey, like a tawny owl, it's a mistake to try and hand rear it yourself. What happens is that you tame it and he becomes what we call an imprinted owl. He can never go back to the wild. He's a bit of a wasted owl really and he becomes offensive to other tawny owls. They beat him up and he flies away to places he shouldn't go. He won't hurt you, son, so don't leap about.' – this to a small boy who is having second thoughts about whether he wants Chestnut to settle too close to him – 'He ate a little boy yesterday so he won't be hungry today. Seriously though, these live on mice, voles, rats and sometimes, in the passion of the hunting during the breeding season, they will take other birds. It's a creature that's never going to be rare. Like the red fox and the grey squirrel, it's a survivor. The eggs of the female are perfectly round, just like ping-pong balls only a little smaller. And they have a clutch of four or five. Sometimes six even. At times they're a bit like humans. They get fed up with their children and they heave them out of their nests too early. They say, "We've had enough of you. There you go. Fend for yourself." And that's when we get them brought in here as an abandoned bird.'

To the delight of the children the little owl gives his characteristic squeak and glides softly between their benches, passing within a few inches of their heads. There is wonder and disbelief on every face; 'When the children come here we've got to teach them to look up occasionally and to watch birds in flight. Not just hawks – everything. It's the most important thing I do here. We're dealing with the next, vital generation and I'd like to teach them that there are things outside pop music and motorbikes. After all, they need to realise that the birds belong to them and are their responsibility. In one sense, they own them. I hope they go away with that message.'

In the misty dawn, Ashley Smith and Jim Chick set out for Salisbury Plain to hunt for rabbits with their falcons. In the car with them they have a box of inquisitive ferrets and two sleek, excited pointers. The men cannot often get away from work together. When they can, this is what they like to do; 'We're off to Bower Chalk and the downs round there. It's perfect country for falconry. Jim's going to fly his Goshawk. She's a large, short-winged bird, ash-brown above, whitish below with closely barred brown lines – and strong as they come. She hasn't got a name, because he doesn't give names to his hunting hawks. She's eight or nine years old and she's one of the hardest birds to fly and to train. She's a sprinting hawk and catches rabbits and pheasants. She'll need to move fast at Bower Chalk because the rabbits all have 'go faster' stripes on them. They come out of their holes going like mad, and it's always good sport because it's very difficult for the hawks to catch them and the rabbits know every step of the way to their next burrow.'

Jim is tall, hard and bearded. His eyes narrow against the light as he faces the steep downland. This is as wild a piece of country as the South can provide. The man looks as though he belongs here. And the goshawk, sitting proudly on his gauntlet, mirrors its master with its stern glance and its pride; 'We spend long hours every week face to face with thousands of people, talking to them and telling them about the birds. Coming out here and seeing the power and beauty of these hawks flying wild and doing the job they've been bred for is an incredible way of relaxing. You'd have to be particularly insensitive not to be impressed by watching them in action. Out here, miles from anywhere and just you and the hawk and the dog, is perfection. Of course, people must have been doing exactly this in this same place for a thousand years and more. But not always for sport. Before gunpowder this was the only way to take birds on the wing. So it was part of everyday life. In those times people would have known all there was to know about hawks. According to his station in life everybody flew the type of bird that was accorded to that position. The guy with the goshawk – probably the yeoman farmer – he was lucky because he was never short of meat. Later on, after guns were invented, hawks became less

Reg Smith displays a Saker Falcon to the left of Jim Chick with a beautiful specimen of an Imperial Eagle at the Weyhill Hawk Conservancy.

fashionable. In Victorian times they were even considered as vermin. Thousands were killed and all were persecuted. Thankfully that's changed today. When we're out here, it doesn't matter to us whether we kill or whether we don't. It matters from the bird's point of view because they are killers by nature. So I'm pleased if the hawk has some success. A measure of success is necessary and important to give it encouragement and to allow it to fulfil its instincts. But for us we judge our sport, not by the amount of quarry we take, but by the splendour of seeing the birds fly. I haven't known anybody come out to watch who was not impressed by them. They are magnificent if they are sat on a fist or on their blocks. But they are beautiful beyond description when they are in the air. They are like perfectly designed and streamlined machines.'

With the venom of an archer's arrow the goshawk leaves Jim's glove and takes a running rabbit in full flight. Its great talons sink into the flesh of the back and its wings are hooded as it protects its prey from anyone bold enough to try and take it away. A ferret's head peeps out of the hole from which the rabbit fled. Then it turns and retreats underground. Almost immediately another rabbit breaks cover and runs for its life. Ashley's slower Harrishawk takes flight and sets off in furious pursuit. As it prepares to pounce, it sees a barbed wire fence close in front of it and just manages to push its weight up and over. That split second delay saves the life of the rabbit. Ashley just about manages to hide his disappointment; 'I don't think that you can consider a bird or an animal in human terms. They don't have feelings like we do – sadness, happiness or disappointment. They think about a very few basic things – eating, sleeping, hunting, more eating and just sitting there most of the time. They don't fly for the fun of it. They fly because it's a necessity. They have to eat. For instance, that big fish eagle back at Weyhill will spend something like 12 out of 24 hours a day sat in a tree. Then, for one hour a day, it will come down and catch a fish and eat it. Birds fly because they have to. The more energy it burns up, the more food it's got to eat. So it pays it to do as little as possible. When we're out hunting it's a bit different because we gee them up. I remember one afternoon when we were out like this but in a large park. There were four or five of us. I had a bird called a Red-Tailed Hawk on my fist. I was very proud of it and enjoyed showing it off to people. We were right on the top of a hill. This bird was a lovely hunter and you could slip her a long distance from the quarry. Well, she sat up high on my glove and looked down. And she could see a hare about a quarter of a mile away. She did a lovely stoop all the way down the hill and very, very fast. Just as she was about to reach the hare it stood up. It was about three feet tall – nearly the size of a donkey. You could have put a saddle on it and rode it if you'd wanted to. Well, the hawk put all her brakes on and landed about a yard from the hare and just stood there. The hare walked round the Red Tail. And the Red Tail walked round the hare. All my friends laughed at me while the two had an eyeball to eyeball confrontation. Then the Red Tail turned back and flew all the way up the hill and landed on my fist as if to say, "Oh no, not me Dad. I'm not chasing that one". I've never seen a sight like that before or since.'

At the Hawk Conservancy Reg Smith is busy looking after the shop while Ashley and Jim are hunting on the Wiltshire chalk. In addition to the crowds, the feeding and all the maintenance work, he has other regular visitors to look after as well; 'Dennis Smith is our vet from Andover. He comes here once a week and has a very important role. Its important because, when you live among the birds as we do, familiarity can make you miss something vital. Dennis comes with a fresh eye and sees anything that's wrong straight away. He also deals with injured birds that get brought in – that's between three hundred and three hundred and fifty wounded birds of prey brought in here every year. They come from all over. We've even had a tawny eagle brought to us from Saudi Arabia with a broken wing. A man who was working out there rescued it from some small boys, who were dragging it down the street on a chain. He took it from them and looked after it for the whole of his tour in the Middle East, which must have been a nightmare. When he was due to come home, he got a licence and brought the bird to us. And it will remain here. It will never fly again. It was too badly injured for that. But it might breed one day with the female tawny eagle which we have. Most of the birds brought in haven't had quite such big adventures. But this week alone we've had a hobby and three buzzards delivered. Two of them came from the RSPCA and one they brought all the way from Wales. In addition to being invaluable to us, I think Dennis has also learnt quite a lot here over the last twenty years. He and his partners are very good at pinning wings, mending legs and they can cope with the problems birds have with their feet and with their lungs, which, with birds of prey especially, can give them a bad time. But the big thing is that it's up to us to keep them fit and well. Exercise is vital, of course, and we keep and fly our birds in the same way as falconers have done for thousands of years in this country. Their diet is also very important. The hawks in the aviaries are fed on a diet of dead chick, rabbit and, occasionally, beef. The vultures have bones to keep their beaks in trim. It's curious that people often ask us about food, but seldom about exercise, which I think is every bit as important.'

While Reg and Dennis do their rounds of the birds, the eyes of the falcons and hawks on their blocks follow every move. Now and again one will stand on tiptoe and shake its wings like a conductor bringing an orchestra to order. Up the drive of a nearby stately home Ashley, meanwhile, is catering for the needs of a film unit. What they are trying to achieve is a slow motion sequence of a Harrishawk in flight and filling the whole screen. Gauntleted hand outstretched, Ashley stands on the back seat of an open Citroen Deux Chevaux. Chris Packham, the cameraman, stands on the front seat, his camera pointing backwards and just above Ashley's right shoulder. His elbows rest on the metal cross-piece and take the weight of the camera. One of Ashley's colleagues holds the hawk by the side of the car. The Citroen sets out down the drive at about 15 mph. When it is thirty yards from the bird Ashley shouts to it and it flies down the drive towards him slowly overtaking the moving car and eventually landing softly on Ashley's hand. After five or six takes, Chris Packham is satisfied and Ashley is glad it is all over; 'We do a lot of this specialist filming – pop videos, commercials – that kind of thing. They're hard work and not an awful lot of fun. People who don't know think it must be great working on a film set. But it's often boring and monotonous. You sit in a car all day waiting. Then you get a call and they say, "Okay, move. You're on in five minutes". You have to dash about and get the birds ready. You might only be needed for half-an-hour and then you're on your way home again. The good film work is natural history material. Then you're working with wildlife cameramen, who understand birds and know their limitations. They're not robots that you can turn on and turn off. They can feel grumpy or tired just like the rest of us. And so they need to be treated properly when they're working. They mustn't be stressed and the film people have to be told when the hawk has had enough. That's when you call it a day. The other plus with Nature films is the locations. It's not whizzing up to London, which I hate. You almost always come to lovely places.'

Ashley strokes the head of the Harrishawk, which seems pleased with the attention. Its eyes swivel upwards as a flock of doves skims the beech trees in the park. It moves restlessly from one foot to the other; 'A lot of people think there is some great secret to training birds of prey. Well, there isn't. Basically, it's just down to hard work and being persevering and spending a long time with them. With us, people see the finished product when the hawk is flying fit and soaring in the sky. It's not the true picture at all. Many hundreds of hours are devoted to training it and getting it to fly that well. What you are trying to do is to make the bird feel as natural as you possibly can, so that it believes it's a wild bird when it's flying. You have to make it look like a wild bird and think like one in its own mind.'

As night settles on Weyhill the calls of the hawks and falcons, the vultures, the eagles and the owls die down. A fox trots round the perimeter fence in search of something smaller and less savage than the birds within. On the hillside above the Hawk Conservancy, where the great fair was held in days gone by, a flock of twenty or thirty herons takes to the air, honking as they go, and flaps towards the safety of the heronry. Peace falls on the Hampshire hills.

THE CHALKE VALLEY

THE Chalke Valley runs from Berwick St John, just to the east of Shaftesbury in Dorset, and ends at Homington close to the south of Salisbury, where the river Ebble, which has formed the valley over the centuries, runs into the Avon. Back into the mists of history this has been known as the secret valley. And the name is appropriate today because, although it is surrounded by some of the most prosperous countryside in the land, it still seems cut-off and quiet and untroubled by modern life. It is at its luxuriant best in June, that most joyful of months, the scenery, the trees, the plants and the fields are in full bloom. Tiny roads thread the valley and the villages are placid and calm in the summer sunshine. Famous men, including Anthony Eden and Cecil Beaton, had their homes here, but it is the unsung people of the area who, through the generations, have left their mark upon it.

ARTHUR Penton lives at Nunton and, in his mid-eighties, is one of the last drowners in the country. His job is caring for and keeping up the water meadows along the great river Avon near Britford. For centuries, drowners, by controlling the water on the meadows, produced high quality early grass for sheep and cattle. Today, nitrogen fertilizer does the same job, while it helps to pollute the water supplies, which Arthur still watches over; 'I started over seventy years ago in these same meadows, just after I left school. I didn't come straight to the meadows. When I left school first – and before I left too – I used to go milking twice a day, 5.00 in the mornings that was. And then in the afternoons too. Next I had about six months helping the gardener at the farm and feeding the fowls. And after that I went out with me father in the meadows. And I've been here ever since. The main thing I've learnt with water is that it's like fire in a way of speaking. It's a good servant. But, if it gets the master of you, you're beat. So you've got to control it the best that you can. The water that we get in these meadows during the summer, that's all right. It helps freshen things up. But in the winter it's different. We get a lot of rain then and it's all running down from the hills and the towns and into the rivers. When it gets down here, see, it's a dirty brown colour. And as that is distributed over the meadow it leaves a certain amount of silt behind. That works in the meadows for the next twelve months. It's the silt what does it.'

Arthur is slim and fit. He has high cheekbones and his eyes are bright behind his spectacles. He bicycles more than four miles to and from work every day. There can be few people in the world who have worked on the same small patch of land for seventy years without a break; 'I can't mind what year it was, but there was a big flood in Salisbury. Shoppers had to walk up the street on planks or be taken up in a boat. It was pretty bad. When you got down to the meadows, you couldn't see a thing. It was just a sheet of water. If you didn't know the meadow it wouldn't be safe to walk out there in waders else you'd be dumped in a ditch. Them times you could find all sorts of things. One day there was washed down a big barn owl in a cage. Stuffed it was. Lovely, light brown colour. I took it home and had it for several years. Then later we found two sheep in the river. Well, we thought of tying them on. But we didn't. We pushed 'em on down and let them go. As father said, "We don't want them dead things hanging about our part of the river." An hour or two afterwards a butcher from Salisbury come out:

"You seen any sheep?"

"Yeah"

"Where are they then?"

"Oh, we sent 'em on down"

"Pity you done that", he said "I'd have given you a pound each for 'un if you'd saved 'un. Didn't die of anything bad. Just drowned. They'd've been all right."

'And I mind a November morning when it wasn't too hot, I can assure you. A lot of mist and fog about. We was in a boat cutting weed. It was one of the deepest parts of the river. And I pulled on the rope and, instead of the rope coming, it was me that went over the tail of the boat. That was cold too. I got out safely, but I'd lost me hat. I was wet already so it didn't make much difference and in I went again after him to get him. Well, I got me hat, went home and changed and I never had a cold.'

The old man gently clambers down the bank into the river. His back is a little bent from years of toil. He wears waders high up on his thighs. In his hand is a heavy wooden scythe; in his pocket a sharpening stone. It's a perfect summer's day. Flowers deck the meadows and the edges of the ditches and the streams. The sound of water is everywhere. Slowly and methodically Arthur starts to cut the weed, which floats downstream in great clumps. There is still wiry strength in the old arms as they swing back and forth with the effortless rhythm of the country; 'We gotta keep the weeds down. No-one would never really believe how the weeds will keep the water back. You can see how they block the water-course. So we gotta do this job. It's just the same with the big ditches out in the meadows. It's surprising, if you didn't trim them out, how soon they get stopped up. It's only nettles and grass, I know. Nobody would never believe it if they hadn't seen it. It may look like hard work but then I ain't done bad on it, have I? I don't think so anyway. I've had eighty-five years and enjoyed every one, which is fair enough I should say. And I don't 'spect there's many feet in these meadows I haven't walked on in that time. Must have trodden on every bit of 'un. Somebody did say to me one day; "What you don't know about it isn't worth knowing." And I said, "Well, perhaps you're right. But I can still learn. It's surprising the things you pick up each season."

'The saddest of all is that the other water-meadows are let go. They won't have nothing to do with them now, see. There should be three more lots of 'un down here beside these. But they've never done nothing to 'un. Just let them go. And there are other changes too – some for the best and some not. Up in the village, I mean years ago, when all the farmers were doing their meadows and had dairies with lots of people working them, then it was all farm cottages. Now there isn't but about two. All the others are sold to people come in from Salisbury and far away living there so they say. All the years I bin up at Britford, I go up there now and it's like going to a strange place as regards the inhabitants. There are just one or two I know and that's all.'

'PAY' Grant farms the downs above Alvediston, where Anthony Eden once lived. She and her family run more than 2,000 ewes on the rich grassland, as well as cattle and some rare breeds of sheep – Soays and Mouflons. 'Pay' had her training as a shepherd in Wales and still finds Wiltshire a little overcrowded for her tastes. But, up on the high and lonely downs, she loves the views and the landscapes – and the work; 'I was six or seven years shepherding in Wales. I loved the hills there. They really cut you down to size because they made you realise how insignificant you were. When I first came here I found it a bit claustrophobic. You can see smoke from other people's chimneys, which I wasn't used to. Over the years, though it took a bit of time, I've grown very fond of this place too. It's a fine valley – peaceful and full of wildlife and flowers. I'm no gardener but I love all the plants you find out on the downs, and the skylarks. Then there's a buzzard which lives up one of the side valleys. So that all adds to the pleasure even if the work is hard at times. The year begins with the lambing, of course, and that's a busy time. But we get extra help then from some students, who sometimes stay on for a bit afterwards. Then there's dosing the sheep, looking after their feet, shearing and dipping. All in all, there's enough to keep us occupied. It's not as tough now as when we used to winter all the sheep out on the downs. It's very bleak and cold in the dark months and it could be hard going in those days. I remember the winter of 1962–63 when the snow was up above the fences and we had cattle and sheep on the hills. We didn't dig our way out to them until 5.00 at night – and it was dark by then, of course. Well, we carved a channel for them just wide enough to get into a field and they lived in that tiny area for a month or more. They had a one-way track to the water-trough and we worked hard that year.'

'Pay' is out on the downs to round up a big mob of sheep and to bring them in to the farmyard. With her is a great, black and brown, New Zealand Hideaway sheepdog, which bounds across the grass and barks furiously, ordering the sheep here, there and everywhere. From a distance the flock makes intricate patterns against the green grass as the sheep break or bunch or form into narrow lines as they fight their way through openings in the fences; 'One thing I think about is that you hear of people spending thousands of pounds buying paintings of landscapes to hang on their walls. Yet, if only they opened their eyes, it's all there for free really, isn't it. If you're lucky enough to live out here you've got all of that and a peaceful, rural life as well. Not so peaceful today perhaps because we've had the ewes in for shearing already. Now we've got to bring them all back to be wormed and treated for foot-

66

rot. We've also got to separate the fat lambs – fit, not fat, we have to call them nowadays – from their mothers, so that they can go off to market. We must have ten or twelve groups like this round the farm, so that's what mainly keeps us busy in between hay-making.'

DENNIS Chalk's name is a suitable one for a man who lives in Broadchalke in the middle of the Chalke Valley. He was village postman for 23 years and is a dab hand at carving walking-sticks. But he really comes into his own when he is conducting the Wilton and District Youth Band, which is much in demand locally and on tours in this country and overseas; 'There's nothing like village life – nothing at all. Things are changing now but, going back to when I was a boy, everyone had to do everything in these small places. It was like a big family. If anything happened in the village – say there was a fire or a serious accident – everybody knew about it and lent a hand. Today, with the children going to school outside the village, it's not the same any more, I'm afraid. But it's still beautiful and so is the valley, of course. As far as the band goes, it started as an idea 25 years ago. The headmaster of the school at Wilton had some instruments laying around. He knew I was interested in

Dennis Chalk, bandmaster of the Wilton & District Youth Band, has been helping local children learn, play and love music for twenty five years.

teaching young people, so we got the youngsters together, shared out the instruments and formed the band, which is still running today.'

On a lawn which slopes down to the Ebble, the band gathers to play to the villagers. Broadchalke church stands proudly in the background. The garden is full of summer flowers and, in the river, trout dart and turn swiftly in the current as they feed. Swallows skim the surface of the water and the evening sun is warm as it glints off the band's instruments. The music echoes proudly down the village street and passers-by stop to listen and to watch; 'We play any kind of music which has character to it. One of our favourites is *The Rural Suite* by Eric Ball, who lives close by in Bournemouth. There's always a story in his work and, for us, this piece represents perfectly the countryside of England and our beloved valley.'

The children's faces are serious as they play. Their cheeks swell with the pressure of blowing. The conductor's arms rise and fall. On a brick wall a cat watches lazily as its tail swings softly in time to the beat.

THIS is notable watercress country and the bubbling artesian wells are cool and clean in the summer heat. Leslie Webb, who keeps honey-bees in the bottom of his garden at Bishopstone, has been working in the watercress beds there for the Barter family for more than fifty years. Today the produce goes as far away as Liverpool, Leeds and Birmingham from this tiny Wiltshire back-water; 'I reckon that the family has been in these parts for nearly 200 years. People live long in this village. Must be something to do with the air I suppose. I always remember folk going on to a good age. The water's good too. That might be something to do with it as well. The Ebble runs by and there are also springs coming up all over the place. In fact there's more or less an underground lake that feeds the springs. At the watercress beds you have to bore down about a hundred feet to get to the water. Then it comes bubbling up and it's just the job. The main artesian well was bored a good time ago. It's a specialist job that, and the water's never stopped running, not even in the worst drought. It may have slowed down a bit but it never ran out.'

Leslie is a small, serious man with white hair and a tanned face. His movements are easy and economical as he works in the cress. The water comes half-way to his knees while he stands in a line with his friends cutting rich bunches of the dark green plant. The knives they use are wickedly sharp; 'This job has changed hardly at all since I first started. There are places where it may be a little more mechanised. But not here because the paths along the sides of the beds aren't wide enough to take runabouts with engines. So we still push barrows to and fro. As for the cutting, that's all done by hand. It always has been and, although they've tried all sorts of innovations, it's been to no avail. It's not been for want of trying though. They just can't do it. Mechanised or not it would still be back-breaking work I promise you. When you get into the packing-house you can straighten up your back again, so that's always a relief after an hour or two cutting outside. When I first began packing up the cress in boxes, each pack had to weigh a quarter of a pound. And we used to put the bunches on the weighing-scales to get them right. You can imagine what a slow business that was. Gradually though we all got used to the size of bunch that made the weight. You could feel it in your grip. I still went on weighing each pack to make absolutely sure. But, after a while, when it was right every time, I stopped. Now, if someone came in I could bet them that every bunch would weigh a quarter pound and I would never be wrong. It looks easy, but it's based on years of just doing it.'

Running water continues to accompany the process in the pack-house. Here you can smell the cress with its rich, clean, tangy savour. Men and women stand opposite each other bunching the plants and binding them with elastic bands; 'I do eat cress but, though I'm ashamed to admit it, I prefer lettuce. It's very good for you this stuff though. It's got iron in it. I can't run it down as a product. It's not to my taste, that's all. You've come in the summer. And it all may look nice and easy. But watercress can be terrible in the winter – there's no doubt about that. You get frosty mornings, so frosty in fact, that you can't start work until it's gone off. You see, if you have frost on the cress, you mustn't push it into the water because it kills it and it all goes black. So you have to be careful. It puts you behind for the whole day and you can miss a delivery that way. You get used to the cold yourself and the freezing water on your hands, just as you get used to the heat. But it's easy for me to talk I must admit, because I don't go out in the beds as much as I used to. I mostly leave that to other people now. They're younger than I am. As for this part of the world, since my family's been here for a couple of centuries, I guess I'll stay put now. I wouldn't want to live anywhere else. I like seeing everything that happens in the village. It's changed more than the cress beds have. They've not altered at all but so many newcomers have arrived to live here that life is different. Agriculture too is not what it was. For me, it's become too mechanised and it's done away with such a lot of workers. But it's no good complaining. We have to live with the times. That's all there is to it.'

At the bottom of his long garden Leslie carefully takes the lid off one of his hives. The bees make an anxious cloud round his head. As he lifts a glistening comb out of its slot, the sun strikes it and it glows golden yellow in the June morning light. The past still seems well within your grasp when you spend the day with men like Leslie Webb.

ROBERT Fry is the Broadchalke butcher and his faggots and sausages are famous up and down the valley. The business goes back four generations in his family and he delivers his meat to all the villages, including the enchanting Ebbesbourne Wake, where his cousin is the landlord of the Horseshoe Inn; 'It's a good enough place to live. I've stayed here all my life anyway and travelled up and down a good few times in my butcher's van. We deliver in the valley twice a week so I get to know most people. I delivered to Cecil Beaton and to Lord Avon – Anthony Eden that was. One day Cecil Beaton's cook came in and wanted veal, which we didn't have. So I took the backbone out of a rabbit, removed the lean pieces and sent her off with them. She did what she had to do with the meat and 'Sir' didn't know the difference and was quite happy. This job's changed since my great-grandfather's time though. People don't eat so much meat these days as they used to. I think great-grandfather used to supply the Pembroke family with quite a lot of large joints every day. But establishments needing that sort of service don't seem to exist any longer. More's the pity for us.'

Robert is a strong, well-built man with black hair and eyebrows. The door to his shop has a double flap. In the sunshine he has the top half open and can lean out watching the village world go by; 'In the old days – before refrigeration – we had a slaughter house behind the shop. Those times they used to kill the beasts one day and sell most of the meat the next. So it wasn't too much of a problem really. They used to smoke meat too. Bacon, of course. But that's a bit before my time. If my great-grandfather came back now, he'd find quite a lot of changes I should say. The freezers of course, and I'm not sure what he'd make of them. Also in the way we cut the meat now and the machinery we use to do it. But, with the faggots, they've barely changed at all. It's mainly pig meat – pigs offal to be exact. And then there's some seasoning and onion. We mix it all up together, cook it and there we are. They're very tasty and very popular too all the way up the valley. People here have had a taste for them for a good few years now.'

The white van cruises slowly up the winding lanes towards Ebbesbourne Wake and its delivery to the Horseshoe Inn there. The best and prettiest by-pass in the country serves this tiny village. It is the narrowest of lanes fringed with summer flowers and just wide enough for two cars to pass one another, provided that they are going slowly. It may spare the hamlet from twenty or thirty vehicles each day. It represents an ideal and rare vision of the English countryside in the modern world; 'The valley hasn't changed much. But the people have. There's not too many what you'd call real locals nowadays. It's not so good people owning houses and not living here all the time – especially if they don't eat meat! But the valley's still good. It's so quiet compared with town life or with some villages with big roads going by them. You can walk up on the hills here – not very far at all – and not see a house or hear a sound.'

GYPSY caravans and horse-drawn wagons have travelled the lanes of the Chalke Valley for centuries. They are as colourful now as ever they were and much of that is due to the artistry of John Pickett who, from his yard at Manor Farm, Berwick St John, and with the help of his wife and father, restores, rebuilds and decorates these venerable vehicles for collectors and travellers alike; 'I came on the scene at the end of an era. It was just when the travellers were changing over from wagons to lorries and trailers. I was lucky enough to overlap with the old times. They ended because the roads changed and so many other things were changing too. It's no joke taking horse-drawn vehicles out on today's roads. What is best about these old caravans is that you can live inside a picture which you have painted. It's

70

A fine fallow buck in winter in the depths of the New Forest – but Dylan Thomas only had eyes for his family:

> 'Out in the dark over the snow
> The fallow fawns invisible go
> With the fallow doe;
> And the winds blow
> Fast as the stars are slow'.

The tranquil River Cerne at Nether Cerne in Dorset. Although the Cernes are most famous for their rude giant, they were once also renowned for their beer. Its excellence was said to come from the purity of the water in the river.

John Pickett restores, rebuilds and decorates old gypsy caravans and wagons, keeping alive an art which had almost become extinct.

better than having a picture on the wall because it provides you with a vehicle and accommodation and your painting all at the same time. That's the idea I started out with and it's developed from there. Then I got interested in the origins of it all – the men who built the wagons and caravans and who decorated them originally. It's an art that has never been catalogued or written down. So it takes a great deal of time to find out about it, because so much of it has vanished now.'

Bare-chested and dressed in shorts John looks like a pirate as he concentrates on the painting of a scarlet and gold sign. He has not shaved for a week and his long, black hair falls towards his shoulders in tangled curls. His face is full of mischief and he laughs a lot at himself and at people who ask him foolish questions; 'There's not very many of us doing this sort of work now. But then there's not really a lot of people that are prepared to weigh out the money for it. What costs is the time involved in doing the job. It doesn't create a lot of customers. What we charge gives us a working living. You'd get a bit more dealing with the buying and selling. But even that's not a great market. What is good is the living, provided that you enjoy the work, which I do. It's to do with peace of mind really and satisfaction with what you are achieving. The caravans themselves are unusual structures. They last quite well as long as they're maintained. They're made of wood and that, of course, is damaged by the elements. The paintwork, the gutters, the roof – there's so much to it that you have to keep on top of it all the time. The sun is as bad for it as the wet is. In practical terms they're an awful construction. They're not sensible at all. They turn the structure of a shed inside out, so the ribs are on the outside and what would be outside is in. It's all done for the 'flash' of the thing if you know what I mean. They're show-off vehicles. The old builders worked to the amount of money people wanted to spend. How much cash you put down was how grand a cart you got in the style of the English, gypsy caravan.'

The yard is full of vehicles in different stages of repair. Round every corner is another multi-coloured work of art. Two big goats graze near a patch of nettles. A cat sleeps on the seat of a golden carriage, which looks like Cinderella's coach. John, high up on a ladder, is chiselling rotten wood from the roof of a big caravan. Nearby, his wife and father are putting the undercoat on the door and wheels of another gypsy home; 'My family helps a lot you know. And not only when it's sunny like it is today. It's handy to have them around. They do all the basics and they do them well. That leaves me free to do the other bits and pieces – good work in the carving and the painting and that sort of thing. But the base work is just as hard as my side of it. My main pleasure is trying to follow in the footsteps of the old boys who actually built these vans. They never had any recognition of what they did and they were brilliant. It's not reproduction really. It's a continuation of their great skills, which were only understood by the travelling people. But it's still alive. It's still there. And I'm proud to be a part of it – just carrying on what they created and laid down.'

THE seventeenth century historian, John Aubrey, had a small farm at Broadchalke in the heart of the Ebble Valley. He wrote of the sounds of the church bells mingling with the sounds of the little river's running water and boldly claimed that 'there are no better trouts in the kingdom of England than here'. Travelling down the dozen or so miles of the Chalke Valley, it is easy to understand the loyalty of Dorset and Wiltshire people for their counties. Here is the England of which the poets write and which the tourists flock to see. Happily, this secret place seems so far to have escaped their notice.

PAMBER FOREST

IT is hard to imagine a Royal Forest just to the north of much-maligned Basingstoke in Hampshire – once a charming country market-town. But such a place was Pamber Forest and much of it remains intact today. It encloses the villages of Tadley, famous for its fights, Pamber End, Pamber Heath, Pamber Green, Silchester, with its Roman wall, and Little London. The rights of the Chase in the forest were abandoned in 1605 after an official inquiry reported that 'there hath been no deere in the Pambeare Forest within memory of man'. It was an area famous for its woodland crafts – rake-making and brooms – and those skills still linger. Many of the local people used to combine forestry with itinerant farming. They often brought in three harvests – in Sussex, at home and in Wiltshire – before returning in the autumn to gather their hops and acorns. They were fiercely independent and clannish. If a man came on the hunt for a girl from outside the forest area a group of Pamber lads would be waiting to knock him about. And, even today, down the forest lanes and in the back streets of the hamlets you meet people with whom you would not want to pick a fight.

THE harvest came early in a sun-scorched summer for Guy Elliot from Frog Lane Farm, Little London. So, by the middle of August, much of his old-time harvesting machinery had been put to bed until next year. But he and his brother were still working their formidable rack saw and thrashing their wheat sheaves to provide straw for local thatchers; 'Cutting the corn with an old-fashioned binder takes up more labour than you would need with a combine. That's obvious and it's why modern farmers favour the combine harvester. Trouble is though that there's not the enjoyment. You sit up there on a machine – and I don't mind whether it's a tractor or a combine. You're on your own and the only person to talk to is yourself. In the olden days everyone cut with a binder like we still do and then afterwards we built the sheaves into stooks. There was a gang of men and you could have a bit of a chat and a laugh and a joke amongst yourselves. It made it all more enjoyable. The reason we still do it this way is because I need straw for thatching. There's quite a demand for it and I enjoy doing it like this. Combines are no good for that job. They chop it all up to nothing. It's got to be long and straight for thatching. And it's got to be wheat straw especially grown for the job.'

Guy and his family have had Frog Lane Farm for 67 years. The yard is a parking lot for venerable machinery and tools of every size and type. Nothing here is for show. Everything is for using. Below the farm house the binder, its sails turning like a windmill, makes its steady circuits of the field. When it has passed by, men pick up the sheaves one by one and stand them up six or eight to the stook; 'Well, I was born at Tadley more years ago than I care to remember. Dunno whether you've heard of the treacle mines. My brother and I was both born there in the famous Tadley treacle mines. The place was called Honey Bottom. Famous for its bees it was. So that's where the name comes from. We moved to this farm when I was away being born. Afterwards, I came back here with my mother. That was in 1922. After I'd grown up and gone to school I've been farming away here ever since. I sometimes think I'd like to have moved. I'd have enjoyed being on the hills somewhere on the chalk clay where you get better cereals. But not now. It's too late. I'm getting on in years and moving might not be so good.'

Above the farm two stacks of last year's wheat sheaves stand thatched against the wind and weather. A wooden thrashing machine stands alongside one of the ricks. Men with pitchforks throw sheaves from the top of the stack to men on the machine, which shakes and judders as it performs its intricate duties. It is belt-driven from a nearby tractor. Grains of wheat pour into hemp sacks at one end. Giant straw bales emerge at the other and, in the middle, the chaff drops to the earth or is whisked away by the wind. An old black labrador, coated in dust and dirt, stands watching with sad, motionless eyes; 'These stacks were put up last summer and we've only just got round to thrashing them now. But the corn and the straw keeps well if you build the ricks properly. This old machine was the starting point for the combine harvesters. This was a brilliant piece of invention. And the people who made the combine found a way to join what this one does to the binder and to do both jobs in one. My brother and I look after all this machinery together. It's a labour of love all right and we've been doing it all our lives. We've never been taught by anyone. Now I buy old relics for parts to keep the working ones going. I pick up stuff where I can. The reaper and binder are just pre-war and the thrashing machine is around the same age. Looking at the modern combine you can see how far things have come in just fifty years. It's the same in the village too. That's altered such a lot. I knew everyone once. Now I hardly know anyone. Nobody's got the time and there aren't the characters around. The pub is different as well, although it's more of a pub than a lot of them are these days. Of course, there was two more pubs in the village before. The next house down from us was a pub and there was another just below the Plough. That was where my father and grandfather were born. We've been around this part of the world for 350 to 400 years farming in Silchester, Mortimer and here. So it must suit us I suppose.'

WILLIAM Rawlings from Tadley is 78 and is known far and wide throughout Pamber Forest. His family is in the scrap metal business but his heart is with his cattle and his horses and in the glades of the local woodland, where he takes delight in driving with his pony and trap on summer mornings; 'Years gone by all the Tadley villagers practically lived out of this forest, cutting broomsticks, bean poles, pea rods, thatching spars, birch bavins for the heads of brooms and everything else you can think of. The Tadley broom-makers were famous and so were our flower

76

women. Our wives and daughters used to collect lilies of the valley, bluebells, wild daffodils, heather and violets out of the copses and we would take 'em to Basingstoke and sell 'em. Practically everyone hereabouts used to get a pick out of Pamber Forest. Them days are gone for good now. And I can't say they was bad days. I'm on about times when you could buy a plot of land in Tadley for £20. It almost belonged to the Tadley villagers this forest and they used to buy it by the acres. When I was a boy there was a grand old man who used to pull the timber out of here. All horse-drawn it was on big timber carriages. You see, I can go back well over sixty years in these parts so there's a lot of memories. I'm still surrounded by family too, though quite a few have gone away – and we just lost a youngster of 84. But I've got grandsons following in me footsteps now and they're good wi' horses like I am. They can't get up to some of the things now which we used to do though. 'Cos we done a smart bit of hare-coursing, rabbitting and other stuff. And the keepers are a bit strict on it. I remembered them old days some of my school-mates were birched for taking eggs off a pheasant. Well, you don't get that for murder today.'

William is a unique old man. Dressed in black cowboy gear, like a veteran Roy Rogers, his face is crumpled with smile lines and burnt by the sun and wind. In a meadow surrounded by forest trees he blows long, cool notes on a cow's horn trumpet, and cattle and horses come trotting across the grass to be fed. Then he harnesses a sturdy Welsh cob and sets off in his cart along the tracks through the woods. Two strong grandsons trail him in another trap; 'We used to do a bit of trotting years gone by. Races, you know. I don't do so much of it now. I'm too old. But it was good fun. I like doing it in more gentle fashion like this nowadays. Them times we used to hobble the horses out on Tadley Common and that was genuine common land. It was quieter too, of course. I can remember when I drove a cart from Tadley to Basingstoke and round to Newbury as well and not pass a car. It was all gravel tracks then. They used to drive the cattle by road from the forest up towards Mortimer and have sales on Mortimer Common. Those days we were living off the woodland mainly. And slowly we got into motor-breaking and scrap. When that began I mind that I could do scrap-iron at Basingstoke Station at eighteen shillings a ton. Nowadays it's about £60 a ton, and the family still carrying on with it. They're still driving through the forest like them times too. To start with we used to foot it from Tadley to the pub at Little London. It's a good thing to be able to do on a Sunday morning to come through here. Better still horse-drawn. And even better if the beer was like it used to be then – fourpence a pint and so strong that, after a couple of pints, you knew you'd been drinking. And cigarettes just fourpence a packet. Then a grand walk home through the forest as happy as can be.'

The two horses pull their loads to a halt beneath the Plough Inn sign at Little London on the edge of Pamber Forest. The red brick walls are weathered and welcoming. The horses begin to crop the shaggy grass while the men disappear through the door into the bar.

THERE was once a Rake and Sneadmakers Union in Tadley – so many local people were involved in crafting tools and hurdles from the wood of Pamber Forest. Today, Arthur Nash makes brooms for Buckingham Palace – and for non-royal customers as well – in almost exactly the same way as his forefathers did a century or two ago; 'Years past there were many, many families in Tadley making these brooms. There was our family, there was the Saunders, the Ramptons, there were the Smiths, the Bowmans, the Wests, the Uppertons, the Gundrys, and more besides. But I'm afraid in the early '60's brooms took a bit of a knock from man-made fibre such as nylon and plastic. A lot of the broom-makers got regular jobs then. Now it's all coming back again and it's booming. But there's not a lot of us left. There's myself, the Saunders, there's West and I think there's a Gundry on the outskirts of the village that makes them still. The reason they're making a come-back is that they're better, they're natural and you can't beat 'em. What they're famous for is sweeping up leaves. There's nothing'll do that job better. When they're worn down a little bit and they're stubby, they are ideal for sweeping your lawn to get all the dead grass and the moss out. They're good too for clearing up snow and hedge trimmings. In other words, they're an all year round broom for all seasons.'

Arthur is a broad, strong man with an open face shining with exertion as he sits astride a wooden block in his shed and works steadily away. It is like a scene for a witches' conference with broomsticks stacked in piles on all sides. Outside a cauldron steams on an open fire and the air is full of the smell of wood-smoke and varnish; 'Before the war we used to use a withy to bind the bundles of twigs onto the handles. They were made of ash, hazel-wood, willow or osier. They were strong enough those thin struts of wood bound around and they did the job. But now I use galvanised wire. It's quicker and it's tighter. Apart from that, they're much the same as they always were. For handles, I've relied on Pamber Forest. I like to use hazel if possible. It's not essential but it's probably the best. There's not much birch round here. What there is grows on the common land and we cut it young – about six to ten years old. That's in the winter when there's no sap in the wood. We tie it in bundles, bring it back, stack it, keep it dry but also keep it so that the air can circulate round it. Otherwise it will go curly. We leave it there for a minimum of six months, maybe longer, and it's ready then for picking down for use. These brooms are also called besoms. I'm told that's a Scottish word for a wayward woman. So maybe that's where the witch comes into it. But, as an industry, it's based here in Hampshire, though there's probably some in other counties too. There's certainly nothing in the North. Ninety percent of the brooms I make go to the London area. There's Buckingham Palace – that's top of the list. Then there's the Royal Gardens, Kew Gardens, the Royal Parks, Wembley Stadium, London Zoo, Kempton Racecourse – these sorts of places buy them. And they always have. Even before the war Tadley folk used to take their brooms nearly always to London. They'd carry them by the cart-load. They'd drive the load down to Aldermaston Station – several loads in fact. Then they'd put them all on the train and themselves drive a full load to London.

Arthur Nash makes brooms from the wood of Pamber Forest, a skill which has been in his family for several generations.

They'd meet the train the other end, stack them up somewhere and then go round delivering to the shops in the London area.'

The work is steady and unrelenting. The strong hands twist and bind, turn and tighten. Nothing is left to chance in the regular rhythm of the process. The mouth and cheek muscles move with and register the effort involved; 'I can make a dozen brooms an hour once all the materials are prepared and ready. I work an eight to ten hour day, so you can work it out for yourself. They'll last well, but you must keep 'em dry. If you're gonna leave your broom outside on the grass it's gonna spoil. If you keep it dry it will last till you wear it out. I was talking to a woman the other day who'd had hers for fifteen years. So they're strong enough. And so am I and all. They say I haven't got blood, I've got sap in my veins. My grandfather Nash did this sort of job but, as far as I know, he never made a broom. He just shaved the handles. They reckon he shaved forty dozen handles in one day, which is something incredible you know. It's two days' work really – forty dozen pointed and shaved. Then there was my great-grandfather Saunders. He would go to London with a load of brooms – twenty-five dozen he'd take. He'd come back two weeks later with sixpence. He'd called in on several pubs on the way home, you see. And he had a big family as well to look after and sixpence didn't go very far.'

AT Ramsdell, Brian Cooper keeps and cossets the mighty Shire horses, with which he has won many prizes at major shows. This is grand country for riding and driving, and the years roll back at the sound of horses' hooves clipping the stones on the gravel forest tracks. But these giants are more accustomed to the smooth turf and the marquees of the show-ring; 'We've had them since the mid-60's, somewhere around that time. We've always been interested in 'em, my wife and myself. They get you away from run of the mill work, especially going to shows. Before we got the pedigree Shires I worked for a while with me uncle with his horses. He owned quite a few working for Hampshire Council and they took a bit of handling. But they're all right when they get used to you. One of our big chaps is called Thumper. We've had him from a two year old. He's been very good. We had him broken at three and have used him ever since in shows and musical drives. Last year a company borrowed him. They took him to Wembley in the heavy horse musical drive and he's never been any trouble. He's a very good teacher too when you've got him teamed up with a younger horse, which is learning. He won't teach any bad habits – only good ones. Fred is our other one. He's only four years old. We broke him in in July and took him to a show straight away. He's got a good temperament. He just wants a little bit more experience. He gets on very well with Thumper and he doesn't take much notice of anything.'

The two great horses tower above their owners as they are groomed, combed and have their fetlocks washed and cleaned. Now and again they nudge at one another with their heavy noses. But their eyes are calm and placid; 'It's hard to believe but it takes at least four hours to get a horse ready for a show. It would take a little more than that if you wanted it really spot on. I generally bath them and give them a wash and my wife does the plaiting of the manes and the ribbons. She's really good at that after all the years she's been doing it. It's satisfying to drive them out through the countryside or round the ring looking so smart. What you need to have when you're driving them is confidence in the horse. That's the main thing and I can generally tell when a horse is going to do anything nasty. Like when he puts his tail down and his ears back, look out. But I never put them in the cart till I'm near enough sure that they're safe. They've got to be traffic proof on the roads. Mind, it's hair-raising in the show-ring sometimes with all the children running around. They don't seem aware of the danger at all. Still, we're used to it, 'cos we've been taking Shires to shows for twenty-one years now and we've had quite a lot of success. But my problem is that, as soon as I've got a horse going well, I'm inclined to sell it. Because the pleasure is training it and getting it right. Where there is less pleasure perhaps is in keeping the harness cleaned and oiled. You can spend hours on that and on the dray too to get it anywhere near right.'

The high, yellow cart, bearing the legend, 'Brian Cooper – Basingstoke', trundles its way along the country lanes. The two Shires do their job effortlessly and with discipline. Bowler hat on his head, Brian surveys the passing countryside from his privileged position on the driver's seat. He talks softly to Thumper and Fred. In his hands the reins move and turn as he sends his urgent signals to the horses' mouths.

JIMMY Williams from Tadley is every inch a showman – it goes back seven generations in his family – and his roundabout and gallopers are a regular sight at local fair grounds. Jimmy paints his panels and ponies in traditional colours and the old organ still plays the brightest of tunes with the help of a local steam engine; 'There can't be many families which can claim to have had a roundabout for as far back as we have and to have gone out travelling with it. Some of the bits and pieces we use go back through the seven generations. But of course the transport has altered. We've gone from horses to steam-engines and from steam-engines to diesel lorries for pulling it around. We take it all over the place – to Stoneleigh up in Warwickshire; we go down to Bristol; and sometimes we head over to Sussex. Anywhere within about hundred miles really. We're always made welcome wherever we go and we're friends with the organisers of all the different shows. But I like to come back home to Tadley after. It's where I was born and bred. I used to know nearly everyone here – though that's changed a bit now. I went to school here. It's exactly a mile from our yard to the school. I walked to school every morning of me life you know.'

Jimmy is tall and dark with piercing blue eyes and a warm smile. A magnificent steam-engine is slowly warming up on the grass in the paddock, getting ready to drive the organ. In the meantime, Jimmy heads for his paintshop where he is busily decorating the horses for his veteran ride; 'It was my father taught me to paint. I've always loved doing it. It is quite complicated but, when you've done it all your life, it

81

Jimmy Williams decorates traditional fairground roundabouts. Driven by steam engines to the sound of a steam organ they are everyone's idea of 'the fun of the fair'.

becomes almost instinctive and you know how it should go. My Dad was a very good painter and I suppose I must get my skill from him. We don't have a family mark or anything. But an outsider, who knows about these things, can go to a traction engine rally or a show anywhere four or five hundred miles from here and he can look at some of the work that I've painted or that the family might have done and he'll be able to say "Jimmy Williams's family painted that". You see, I do a lot of blending. I draw one colour into another one. Another painter does the same, but he don't do it quite so much as I do. I don't say he don't do it as good as I do, but not quite so much blending. That's how you can tell it's a Williams.'

Outside in the sun the steam is up and the organ begins to play its strident and evocative tunes. All of Tadley is entertained by the sound. The great instrument is lavishly decorated with Williams pictures and patterns. The steam-engine beside it is immaculate in green and black with shining brass; 'The organ goes with the roundabout and we're just trying it out today. They're very temperamental these things. When it's hot weather they're a real difficult job and they go out of tune easily. We put cool water round them wherever we can and that helps a bit. We're lucky in the village here because there's an organ-maker of all things. He was a schoolteacher before and he took up the organ business. He's building some new ones and he came up the other day to tune ours. It would be easy enough, I suppose, to put an electronic box of tricks in the middle of this old shell. But I don't think the public would fall for that really. They know the sound of the traditional organ when they hear it and they love 'em. That's why, in my opinion, they'll go on. They must go on forever. Before the war there was only one organ man, I think, doing repairs, cutting music and tuning. Now there's a new generation that have learnt the music trade. I should think there must be twelve to fifteen organ men now and it's no trouble to get any repairs done or even to have a new organ built. It's different with the gallopers mind. There's not a handful of really good wood-carvers today that is willing to do that class of work. It takes up so much time. I've got one I can go to if anything breaks or he'll make me a new panel. But they are few and far between and very expensive too I'm afraid. All I've got to worry about now is how the business will carry on. I'm the only one left. I was the only child that got married. I had a daughter. She married outside the business and she's not interested in it, I'm afraid. So, I don't know. I just don't know. It's a sad, old story really and we'll just have to see how it works out.'

IN 1791 Gilpin wrote of the people in this now threatened part of the North Hampshire countryside; 'Their business is to cut furze and to carry it to the neighbouring brick kilns — for which purpose they keep a team of forest horses; while their collateral support is deer stealing, poaching or purloining timber. In this they are said to be expert; that in a night's time they would have cut down, carried off and lodged safely in the hands of some receiver, one of the largest oaks of the forest. From their earliest youth they learn to set the trap and the gin for hares and pheasants; to snare deer by baiting hooks with apples from the boughs of trees and to single out fat bucks with firearms.'

THE CERNE VALLEY

THE winter months are probably a sensible time to visit the Cerne Valley in the heart of the Dorset downland and a half dozen miles to the north of the county town. In the fair weather, this stretch of superb rolling country is very much on the tourist beat and the villages can be crowded and confined. In the quiet cold of December, there is time and space to enjoy and appreciate the breath-taking vistas and the old world charm of deepest Dorset. Cerne Abbas was once the largest market town in the area. Locals tell you that the early postal address for their neighbouring town used to be Dorchester near Cerne Abbas rather than, as now, the other way round. The village was famous for its leather goods, its smuggling and its beer. The water from the river Cerne was so pure that the brew was said to be superior to all others.

Of course, what draws the crowds to Cerne Abbas is not the beer or even the old abbey ruins, the classic countryside or the welcoming people and pubs. It is the world famous giant etched in chalk in all his majestic virility on the hillside above the village. In Thomas Hardy's *The Dynasts*, Mrs Cantle mentions this extraordinary figure when she launches a diatribe against Napoleon and his potent powers; 'I can tell you a word or two on't. It is about his victuals. They say that he lives upon human flesh and has rashers of baby every morning for breakfast – for all the world like the Cernel Giant in old, ancient times.' Today, the great creature stands peacefully on his downland patch, disturbed only by sheep and cattle and by passing helicopters with photographers on board. He is still reputed to offer fertility by strange and magic means to local ladies.

NIC Hill and Pauline Holland live at Minterne Magna, where the river Cerne rises and the valley begins. Nic is a shepherd, responsible for twelve hundred sheep, which graze the surrounding downland. At Christmas time, unseasonal lambs are braving the freezing weather and are giving Nic, Pauline and their dogs enough work to do to keep them all out of most mischief; 'This time of the year we've just finished some of the lambing. We've tried a little experiment for the first time this November. We've had a hundred of the ewes with their lambs outside on this farm to see if it's going to work. So we're busy feeding them and keeping an eye on them. We have four hundred more to lamb early in the New Year and then seven hundred and fifty more in March. So we're mainly on the run, chasing around, doling out grub and trying to keep warm. The lambs are pretty strong, even if they do look small and vulnerable. They're doing all right. They're growing well. They're a lot tougher than I am anyway. I suppose there's some risk involved in having them in this very cold weather with the possibility of snow. But I'm not particularly worried. The mothers have got plenty of feed in front of 'em and their milk is good as a result. So we're just keeping our fingers crossed and hoping for the best.'

Nic is handsome, bearded and calm as he drives his three-wheeled bike up the steep banks to where the sheep are sheltering from the icy wind, which is blowing from the north-east. It is cold enough for the sound of sleigh-bells. Pauline and the collies perch precariously on the vehicle as it shakes and shudders its way up to the waiting flock; 'It may be hard this life. But it's beautiful too – especially here in Dorset. It's something to do with the light and the shape of the hills and the shadows. Going west this is probably the first county where you get civilised countryside. There's downlands in Hampshire and Sussex. But not the variety which you get here. All right, it can be cold, wet and miserable. But I enjoy being out in the open air. Most of the time I'm my own boss. It's different every day, working with the sheep and the dogs. There's little monotony or repetition. And you're always learning something. Anyway, I don't like central heating very much. Some people say that sheep are stupid and that it must be frustrating working with them. Well, yes they can be silly creatures. So can human beings. But sheep are quite intelligent when it comes to survival or self-interest. They can find their way around all right and they look after their own. If there's a hole in a fence or a weak place in a hedge, the sheep will find it soon enough. They'll be through it in no time. They'll always find the better grazing on the far side of the fence if it's reachable. They're always on the look-out for better things for themselves and for their lambs.'

In a green meadow, close to where the river Cerne begins its journey to the sea, Nic arrives to look over a bunch of three hundred ewes, which are grazing peacefully in the sharp winter sunshine. The three collies leap self-importantly from the back of the small pick-up and race round the outside of the pasture, pushing the flock together and driving it towards where the shepherd is standing. It is a triumph of remote control, man and dogs in perfect unison; 'I sometimes say rude things about the dogs, but it's only in fun. As far as they're concerned, I'm one of them. But I'm the leader of the pack. It's true that they're doing what they're told. But they're working by instinct, exactly as they would do if they were still in their wild state. They're highly intelligent, of course, and, when they first start out on this job, they quickly pick up what's going on and what they have to do. It would be very difficult indeed for me to manage my work without dogs. It would take me ten times longer and I'd be very frustrated. The good thing is that they enjoy what they do – otherwise, they wouldn't be as enthusiastic as they are. The same goes for me too – and, I think, for Pauline. I wouldn't dream of being a shepherd if it didn't give me pleasure. All right, it can be a lonely job. But there's more people about now than there used to be. It's not the same as it was in the old days when you were up in the hills for evermore with your caravan, and didn't see anybody from week to week. I go home every evening and I can go down to the pub. So I see as many people as I want to – sometimes more. And I see a good many sheep as well. It might sound impossible for one man to keep an eye on twelve hundred and fifty sheep. But it's not as bad as it might seem nowadays with good dogs and a reliable bike that gets me from 'A' to 'B' pretty rapidly. And then Pauline helps me a fair bit, particularly at busy times such as lambing, dipping and shearing. All the odd occasions when I need it, she's there to lend a hand, which also means that the job's not as isolated as it could be otherwise. She may not look that strong, but she can still put in a hard day's work, and find enough energy to get me a cooked dinner every day'.

As the sheep turn and swirl round the shepherd and the dogs watch their every movement, a great buzzard floats overhead, the sun lighting up its pinions as it glides across the valley. Nic's eyes stay with the sheep and each individual animal gets his attention before he turns away and heads towards the high ground.

CHARMINSTER is at the southern end of the Cerne Valley close above Dorchester. The New Inn there is a favourite watering hole for veteran Dorset farmer, Jack Miles, and for his venerable steam engine, which he cares for with as much love and attention as he does for his sheep and cattle; 'It's a nice drop of beer at this pub, ain't it? Love a drop of beer, I do. That's why we come along so often. The steam engine may not be the fastest way to get here but she's sure enough. She was built in 1901 – a few years before I was and she's travelled all over the shop since then – Suffolk, Hertfordshire, Sussex, and last of all here in good old Dorset. Father always had steam locos. And years ago I was all the time playing around with 'em as a boy. We used to keep about twenty-one cart horses down here at one time. Course, then we had to get a bit mobile look. Cos the 'orses was a bit too slow. When we got the steam engine they done away with three or four cart horses straight away. The 'orses just couldn't do the same job of traction as the steam engine look.'

Jack is short and stocky with a beaming, red face. His voice is full of the sounds of his county. Looking at him, you might think that he would be old-fashioned; 'No, I wouldn't go back to them days now, not for nothing I wouldn't. Not when you can get up in a tractor, press the button and drive away in your heated cab. Cor bless you, no. We don't mind playing about with the old steam engines now, but we don't want to go back to 'em for work no more. Mind you, it was a marvellous machine in its heyday look. But then you could afford to have a lot of people to work around it. If you went thrashing, you wanted two men on each engine look. Then you had seven men round each thrashing machine – two up top on the stage, two on the cart rick, one on the sacks at the back, one on the chaff and dust and two at the top of the straw rick. Then you had to have three or four old 'orses pulling the carts look. And it all added up to a tidy sum. We drank cider them days mind. Not beer. And there was a lot of that needed too. Now that I'm retired – 'bout five year ago it was – I prefer to come up here for a drop or two of beer. I went on working – driving trucks and so on – until I was sixty-nine. Now I lets the others get on with it and I enjoys meself.'

At the family's Haydon Farm on the outskirts of Charminster, Jack's brother Harold keeps up the steam theme with a magnificent fairground organ, the sounds of which have echoed across the Dorset hills for many decades: 'I was born in this village seventy-three years ago I should say. And no, I wouldn't change this life for anything. One thing I wanted to do all me life is own an organ. But it took me a long time to get one. About twenty years ago I got this one off of a great friend of mine at Gillingham. It's a beautiful thing all right, but it takes a tidy bit of looking after. You don't know the work to get it out and going on a cold, damp December day like this. We ain't got it real right yet from a long way cos the bellows takes us a couple of days anyway to make good, playing about with the valves on it and one thing and another. Trouble is they're very temperamental weather wise. Whether it's too hot or too cold, it always upsets it. It's even worse than a woman and they're bad!'

Harold is big, tall and cheerful, a rambling mountain of a man. But his great hands are gentle as they start the machine and carefully feed the stacked cards into the music-maker; 'I haven't done so much of it this last twelve month. They really want to be played every week to make a real tip-top job you know. In them days on the fairgrounds they'd start her up and get her right in the spring of the year and then they'd go right round to Christmas, wouldn't they? It was the only music they had really in the old times and it helped keep 'em jolly.'

The music, with a slightly uncertain note, echoes off the old farm buildings. Dorset Horn sheep raise their symmetrical heads to listen briefly before ducking them down again to graze. Charminster church, with the Cerne flowing past, stands proudly at the bottom of the meadow, its old stone reflecting the cold light of evening. Its own music can be heard in the Miles family fields on a Sunday. While the two brothers keep their steam machines in trim, their sister, Olive, who looks after them in their rambling, grey-stone farmhouse, is busy feeding and looking after her ewes and lambs. Everything is peaceful and tidy as night settles on the valley.

DAVE Fox's ancestors have lived in these hills for centuries. His skills as a builder, stone-mason and flint wall expert can be traced back through generations of Dorset craftsmen. He gathers his flints from an ancient tumbledown barn on the bleak summit of Sydling Hill close to the west of Cerne Abbas. When his load is full, he heads back to the village to do some repair on a Cerne house with the comforting name of Old Mount Pleasant; 'We're up in the Dorset heights where I gather me flints. It's about eight hundred feet up and blowing a gale so you can hardly stand up. This line of hills is said to run from Bridport in the west right through to Shaftesbury in the north-east. This old barn has just run into dereliction. They simply let it tumble down. It was one of them old thrashing barns, open at both ends. They used to keep their tackle in it and they could drive in one end and out t'other. It's a tidy place for flints and very useful to me. We've all got our secret areas where we find these stones from. We keep them from one another. And this one is mine. As far as the work is concerned, I think that you've got to pick up the skills as you go along. Every different tradesman's got different ideas. Chaps I used to work with – the old-timers – they used to say; "If you pick a flint up, don't put it down. Use it."

87

Dave Fox stands by one of the flint walls he builds so expertly in the true Dorset style.

Because, when they used to build the garden walls they used to have a big heap of flints with about three times more than they'd ever need. So, best flints went front of the wall, not so good ones back of the wall and all the rubbish went in the middle. There was some use for every piece, you see.'

Dave is strong, red-faced and sturdy. The wind howls about him as he chips away at the stones, neatly splitting the big ones and revealing their shiny, blue-black insides. His movements are neat and economical as the chips of stone and the sparks flicker and fly. The sky is almost the same colour as the lighter flints; 'If I was sensible I would be wearing goggles and a helmet for safety. The old-timers used to have like a pair of goggles – leather with slits cut in 'em – so, if any flint hit them, it wouldn't damage their eyes. There was no glass to shatter or anything like that – just leather guarding their eyes. Of course, you only need that when you're chipping the stone, not when you're laying it in. The house I'm working on down in the village is built in about 1760. That was just about the time they were going from flint to brick courses. A bit before the end of the century they went to all brick. But I'm bringing back the flint again now. A lot of others are too. Most of the Cerne houses are brick with some flint work added. You go round the village and the surrounding places now and a lot of them are coming back the old way with a mix of flint and brick. The secret of laying flints is how you point them in. A lot of chaps fill them out to full with the mortar. They don't show the stone off. See, what it is, your stone is your feature – not your cement and not your brick. I do my pointing with just an ordinary bit of sacking. I rub away at the damp cement and it gives you that old, rough look.'

One of Dave's infrequent jobs is making good the chalk outline of the great Cerne giant; 'I've worked on that job three times in me life now. They have a specialised firm come in when you re-chalk it, which is about every ten years. The last time was 1979 and I think we shifted something in the region of about ninety tons of chalk. We dig out the old chalk all the way round the figure and it's dumped. That all has to be done by bucket. We build like a miniature railway running down over the steep bank and over the face of the Giant. We dig out the old chalk for a depth of about eighteen inches and then it's renewed with lumps of chalk first and the last six inches is like a dust chalk. One sad thing is that we don't use our local chalk, because they said the last time that it wasn't white enough. So we had to bring it all in from Shillingstone.'

As the storm rages over the darkening Dorset hills, the great figure of the giant stands impassively on the downs watching over the people in the village below.

CATHY Goodfellow is the daughter of Bob and Mary Stenhouse, whose cattle graze the rough ground beside the Cerne giant. Cathy and her husband breed and milk Friesland sheep at the family's Francombe Farm on the outskirts of the village. Then she and her mother make delicious cheese and yoghurt, which are much in demand from local people; 'We were too small an outfit to milk cows, so we decided we'd have a go at sheep instead. The Frieslands are a special milk breed and they're quiet and placid as well. They train very quickly. We bring them in when they first arrive and, within a week, they're coming through the parlour – no trouble at all. They don't panic when you're working with them. You get them into a pen and, in five minutes, they're all laid down. They don't seem to worry about anything.'

Cathy is tall and fair with an open country face and a touch of Dorset in her voice. Her blonde hair is tied back with a blue scarf and she works confidently and swiftly in the small dairy, which stands beside the milking parlour. Everything is spotlessly clean. Outside a flurry of snow drifts past the window; 'English cheeses were once made from sheep's milk almost entirely. Then, for one reason and another, they moved on to cows' milk. Now I hope that the trend may be coming back to sheep again. It's much easier and better for cheese-making 'cos you get a much higher yield of cheese for your milk. It's much richer milk altogether. The hard cheese takes three days to make and four weeks to mature. Soft cheese also take three days to make but they're ready to eat after another three days. We sell some from the farm and the rest in local shops. We haven't really looked for any bigger markets than that. A shop in Dorchester and Sherborne keep us going and one in the village. We're milking thirty-five sheep now and they're in milk for five months each year – perhaps five and a half. We freeze all the surplus milk and, when we start to get near the end of their milking period, we begin defrosting what we've saved and using that.'

Two big white cheeses, the size and shape of those heavy weights which Scotsmen push across the ice in their game of curling, are being sewn into neat cloth bags by Cathy's mother. Next door Kevin Goodfellow is cleaning out the parlour while the sheep wait patiently in the yard to be let back into their meadow. Cathy, meanwhile, bustles about pouring yoghurt and soft cheese into containers and cutting cauldrons of white cheese into squares with a kitchen knife; 'I've heard of people making butter from sheep's milk and I'm sure it would be good and rich. But it would be too expensive for people to buy. So I stick to yoghurt and cheese, which are known sheep products. I eat a lot of it myself and so does the family. The children like the hard cheese and the yoghurt more than the soft cheese, which is probably a bit of an acquired taste. Of course, without the good grass in the Cerne Valley, we wouldn't be anywhere. We don't run the sheep on the hill beside the giant – that's where the cattle are. The sheep stay in the meadows below because we have to walk them everywhere, so they have to be close and handy. During the summer they come down the road to the farm each day for milking. It's a lovely sight.'

TOM Sheppard and his wife, Molly, live in Duck Street, Cerne Abbas and carry on a thriving cottage industry of their own making wooden toys, skittles, mats, cribbage boards and rocking-horses. Tom even carpenters prayer stools for the nearby Franciscan Friary beside Batcombe Hill. He gets his wood from a merchant in the village with the picturesque name of Mr Trim; 'When I was a small boy we used to visit an aunt in Lincolnshire. There wasn't much for a child to do in those days – it was in the 1920s – no television and not even a radio. There was a joiner in

Tom and Molly Sheppard in their workshop. Retirement led to a new career in traditionally made toys and rocking horses at Cerne Abbas.

the village called Mr Barton and I used to go across the street to watch him at work and to help him if I could. He hadn't a scrap of machinery of any sort. Everything was done by hand. Occasionally I was given the spoke-shave or some other tool and I just loved every minute of that. And I think that's where the seeds of my interest in joinery were sown. I suppose it started seriously during the war. I made furniture for the children, bookcases, a bed, a toy castle and one thing and another. I got more and more interested in woodwork. I'd never had any formal training and it wasn't my profession. But eventually, when I got near to retirement, Molly and I said to one another; 'Now look, what are we going to do next?' So we decided to go into woodwork production. First I went to the corner shop in Cerne Abbas and told them that I had a lathe and could make little wooden bowls for them. They said; "Oh, yes please". So the owner put the bowls in his window and they began to sell. Then one day a lady came along and asked me to make some furniture for her. Next it was toast racks for somebody else. And almost all the things I have made have been on request. At the friary, for example, they want crosses. They have four different sorts that they need. Certainly I would never have made those unless I'd been asked to by the monks. They have a shop there too to raise money to help them in their work looking after travellers. We went to the friary one day, Molly and I, and walked in the shop. We saw Brother Patrick, who was the Bursar then, and said; "You know, we could make you some wooden bowls and toys and other things for your shop." And he was pleased and agreed. Since then, we've never looked back. Now they take everything I make and it's marvellous what they sell there. We never cease to wonder. When we go over we take them a load of stuff and Bobby at the shop brings out his bit of green paper with a big new order on it.'

The small workshop is neat and tidy. Tools stand in ordered rows. Molly sits intently burning pictures of the village onto wooden mats with a red-hot poker. Tom is hard at work on the hind leg of a rocking-horse. Wood shavings float to the floor and the smell of timber is in the air; 'Soft wood I get from a mill at Middlemarsh which makes pallets. They need pieces of wood about four feet long. If there's a knot in it or if it's warped, they discard it. I take from them the pieces that I can use and make egg-racks from them. Then there's Mr Trim here in the village. He's come up from nothing there. It was a garage and he started to do woodwork when the garage wasn't paying too well. He's doing fine now. He gets government contracts and uses a lot of good wood. I benefit from that because, if there's a piece that isn't quite as it should be, they daren't use it and I get it and can cut out the bit that isn't right. Then there was a lady in Cerne recently had a tree blown down. It was called a Lawson Cypress, beautiful wood, and I've sawn it up into little strips and turned it into dice and other things too. It's red wood and such a rich colour – very satisfying to work with. And so it's gone on. I've made a lot of mistakes, of course – a lot of trial and error. I think my work's improved over the years. I certainly hope so. I should have been a very poor workman if it hadn't.'

In a room at the top of the house, smelling sweetly of the apples which sit on shelves at the far end, are rows of colourful toys and games waiting to bring joy to a hundred children at Christmas. The work is polished and professional, but also shows clearly the love and care which Tom and Molly put into it.

YOU are never in any doubt about when you are in Dorset – such is the unique beauty of this special county. H. J. Massingham, that great recorder of the English downland, came to the Cerne Valley before the last world war and wrote; 'A kind of spell there is in Dorset. The chalk loses more and more control over the shapes of its hills until once more, at Cerne, its naked serenity is restored. Cerne Abbas itself is exceptional among Dorset chalk villages. It is unusually lavish in half-timbering, while the combination of black flints with light stone and gables reminds you of the best village architecture of Wiltshire. Behind the village the famous Giant is carved out of the turf, almost upright for his one hundred and eighty feet of length upon the almost precipitous bare slope.'

Probably these hills have changed hardly at all since the 1930s when Massingham came here – and for centuries before that as well. And this is the greatest charm of Dorset. It is still far enough separated from what modern man is pleased to call civilisation to retain much of its dignity and its solitude.

THE WINTERSLOWS

THE three Winterslow villages – East, Middle and West – lie close to the borders of Hampshire and Wiltshire. Salisbury stands a half dozen miles to the west and this is a straggling country area with hamlets, woods, lanes, farms and hedges all jostling for position. Tickner Edwardes hitch-hiked through the Winterslows in 1909 and wrote, 'Between the villages I met not a soul and saw no living thing but birds and rabbits. It was only two or three miles but I spent a good two hours in covering the distance. I found that, by walking on the soft turf under the hedgerows, I could get along quite silently without bestowing any care on the matter, and so came upon many a familiar but perennially interesting thing. I remember this lane chiefly for its abundance of scarlet berries, and the amazing strife of the birds around me as I went. One would have thought that where there was such a great plenty of food for all comers, each would take his fill in peace. But this was not so. The lane was like a battle-field. I moved in a continual hubbub of aggression. Creeping along under the shady side of the hedge I was in a constant whirl of fluttering wings and vociferous music. Blackbirds charged clattering out on every side, wild with excitement. Song-thrushes darted hither and thither. A cloud of smaller birds – finches for the most part – swept on before me, rending the air with their various notes of combat or alarm. And above it, and through it all, the harsh, grating battle-cry of the missel-thrush pealed out. He, indeed, was the prime cause of all the disturbance . . . . Before I had been there five minutes I set the Winterslows down as a place where it never snowed nor gloomed nor blew cold. I give it eternal sunshine unquestioningly, just as surely as I know that the sky above it is always of the same cloudless blue.'

The January of 1990 might have shattered some of Mr Edwardes's illusions about the weather. But, happily, he would still have discovered people of character and courtesy as he tramped these ancient lanes.

BENTLEY Wood is said to be the last remaining stretch of the primeval forest which used to reach from the South Coast to the Thames Valley. It borders the Winterslow villages and is tended with love and skill by woodman Geoff Parfitt, from Whaddon near Salisbury. His work may look romantic, but in January it is cold, hard and unrelenting; 'I've been out in the weather all me life and I'm used to whatever it throws at me by now. I was born in Somerset, near Shepton Mallet, and I moved up here when I was ten. I lived with me grandparents in the New Forest and went to school there. Then, twenty years ago, when I got married I moved to Wiltshire. I believe it's true that my great-great-grandfather used to drive traction engines doing the forestry work in the New Forest. So you could say that it's in me blood, I suppose. There are those who might think that it's cold, dark and lonely out here in the woods. But it's the sort of life I've always been used to. I've worked on farms too, milked cows all hours of the day and night, done all sorts of land work – and that's uncomfortable and solitary too. So you get accustomed to working on your own and then you come to like it. Well, before long I thought I could see the red light coming for the dairy industry. So I got out and came into forestry. From the New Forest to Bentley Wood wasn't such a big jump.'

Geoff is dark and wiry as he works methodically in a big clearing. A huge fire blazes at the centre and, first by hand and then with the fork-lift on the back of a much-used tractor, he carries branches and undergrowth from the edges and piles them on the flames. Blue smoke drifts through the branches of the trees and blends swiftly with the dark winter sky. The heat is intense and the noise of the crackling timber brings memories of camp-fires long ago; 'It's a great big chunk of woodland this, very close to the hustle and bustle of Salisbury. Yet here in Bentley Wood you have all the peace and quiet of true countryside. I can work away and enjoy everything that is going on around me. It's planted as a commercial wood and that needs to be a success. But it's also interesting for its natural history – butterflies in their season, deer, birds, foxes, badgers. All the things you'd expect but none the worse for that. I think my favourites are the dormice. They're not common and there's not that many people doing much for them. I was fortunate enough, when I was cutting down some trees, to find a couple of them. I always remember. It was in June. It was a dull sort of day. I cut down this tree and, at the bottom, there was a nest with a dormouse curled up in it. I put it in me truck while I had me lunch at 12 o'clock. And the sun came out. I went to let it out again and it ran straight up me leg, up on to me shoulder and then on up a tree I was beside. From that day on I took a real interest in dormice and, because I like 'em and because they're protected, I try to look after them in the wood and the places they live. That's particularly important this time of the year when I'm clearing up. There's no birds nests about, but you have to keep your eye open for any other creatures, which may be tucked up for the winter. We've got clearings to clean and patches to tidy and to burn up. It's a general tidy up really in time for the spring. And I'm cutting firewood and stacking that to season on for next year. And all the time watching what's going on in the woods around. So, although the work is hard, there's a lot of pleasure to be had as well.'

As the rain begins to fall steadily and the big drops bite and hiss as they hit the burning wood, Geoff walks across the clearing and disappears into the darkness of the trees. Nearby a cock pheasant shouts a warning and scuttles for cover.

TUESDAY is market day at Salisbury. Even in the first week of the New Year there is plenty of bustle and activity as farmers begin to get their production lines into gear again after the long break. The Annetts family are the Winterslow cattle hauliers and Chris and Bill, his father, are hard at work looking over the livestock and transporting animals to and from nearby farms; 'Tuesday is an important day for us because it's market day at Salisbury. We're here every week, bringing local stuff in from places round the villages and then taking it back out again afterwards. My family's been doing this work since 1921. My grandfather started the business round the Winterslows with horses and carts. And it's changed a lot over the years of course. But the market's still doing the same job. It's a bit quiet so close to New Year, but it'll pick up again by next week. In the days when the firm used to use horses, before I started that was, they were bringing two cows and their calves to market one day. Them times they used to put the calves in the back of the cart and the cows used to walk behind. Well, they got as far as the outskirts of the town – quite a long journey already – and one of the cows, instead of staying with her calf, turned round and ran all the way back into the town centre again. So they had to come back to where they'd started from and begin the journey all over. It was a hard and difficult job in those days and it took them a very long time to get anywhere at all. I enjoy the work now, but I doubt that I would have done then. It would have been too slow for me.'

Chris and Bill watch closely as the big animals enter the ring and march round in circles on the straw. The bidding is brisk and the voice of the auctioneer rises and falls with the pace of the bids. Outside, in the chill afternoon, the smart, blue lorry waits for its next load; 'Even in my lifetime the design of the lorries which we use as hauliers has changed. I can first remember, like when I was small, they used to have to put the sides up on the lorries and to fasten them. It wasn't a container like it is now. They used to put sides on and a tail-board to keep the cattle in when they were hauling them about. In spite of all the problems I can't ever remember one animal escaping in all these years. So we must be doing something right. It's a help to have me dad along on market days with all his experience. There's still a good few of his friends around – the old-stagers, you know – but they're getting less and less, I'm afraid. But he likes to come along and chat to the ones that survive and to remember the old days. As for me, I love this job. I wouldn't do anything else. If I had my life again, I wouldn't change it. I'd still carry on doing the same things. I love working with animals too. Once you've learnt what they're going to do, how they're going to behave, you can get a lot of pleasure out of the work. You very seldom have to manhandle they. They've got four legs and normally, if you treat 'em right, they'll use 'em. As for the Winterslows, I wouldn't want to live anywhere else – certainly not in the town. It's a strange, spread out community and we live right on the outskirts. It's quiet and peaceful even though it's grown no end since I was a boy. As children we used to know everybody that lived in the village. But now we don't know all the ones who live in our road. I still wouldn't swap it though, no, nor the work neither.'

Dusk falls and the father and son slowly drive a score of young animals through the market lanes and up into the waiting truck. There is a scuffle and a scamper as the heavy beasts climb the steep, strawed slope of the tail-board. Soon, with a throaty roar, the lorry sets off on its last journey of the day.

THATCH is all the rage today and men and women with thatching skills are making a sturdy come-back. The Hewletts are the Winterslow thatchers and Lionel, his sons, Chris and Steve, and his daughter, Anna, have done up the roofs of many of the local houses. In January, the family is giving the full treatment to Kyte Croft Cottage at Woodfalls on the north-west edge of the New Forest. Steve is the family spokesman; 'Thatching's been a way of life in my family now for three generations. I learnt off me father and he learnt off me grandfather and we all get on really well together. We work as a team. My family's lived in the Winterslows since the 1940s – just after the war – when grandfather moved to the village. Ever since then we've carried out the thatching business from there. I've lived there all me life and it's a good place to be. I hope one day that I can build a cottage in the village – and it will have to be thatched, of course. There are lots of good, old characters in the Winterslows. I admire them very much and learn a lot from them.'

Steve is a strong, handsome fellow, fresh of face and broad of body. He is outgoing and cheerful. As he and Chris work patiently on the roof, their wood spars for pinning the thatch down and holding it firmly are being made with effortless speed below; 'David Parsons makes the spars for us. He comes from Farleigh and

Lionel Hewlett and his sons Chris and Steve are Winterslow's thatchers, seen here by an example of their beautiful work.

97

he's a great chap. We buy all our spars from him for one reason only. That's because he makes really good ones and they go into the roof smooth as anything. To you a spar may be just a pointed stick. To us it's a vital part of our work. Especially on the ridge of the roof you need good, strong ones. There's a lot of 'em you can buy that aren't up to much. So we rely on David a lot for the quality of his work. You might ask why we don't make our own spars. I can make 'em all right, but we like to stick at one job what you're best at. To try and do two jobs doesn't really work. I wouldn't do either thing well if I was to sit down for a few hours to make spars and then to climb the ladder and start thatching. David makes spar-making look easy because he does it every day of his life, like I do thatching. It becomes a way of life. He picks up a bit of hazel and makes it look as simple as I do when I pick up a bundle of straw. We both handle these things every day and so we make the job go well and smoothly.'

The roof the boys are working on is big and complicated. Wings join the main house. Dormer windows jut from the thatch with difficult curves and angles. And the wind tugs and tangles the loose straw as they struggle to put it in place; 'I started thatching when I left school at fifteen. It's a job which you need to be quite strong to learn and you want to be the sort of person who badly wants to get on and learn how to do it. It's no good if you don't care too much either way. You've got to be someone that can foresee a finished job – like an artist I suppose. He's got to see an old cottage where it's all rough and run-down and be able to imagine in his own head how it's going to be changed. A full apprenticeship for this job would be five years, I imagine. I know a lot of people today would say that that's too long in any trade or profession. But I think you need that time to learn properly. I've been at it nearly ten years now and I'm still learning all the time. There's always new obstacles and problems to get over and they make you scratch your head once or twice. But, one way or another, you've got to get round them. Straight work is the easiest. It's the ridging which is the most awkward and the eaves. Anything decorative or unusual in an old cottage. That's what tests you and that's the first thing people look at, of course.'

The ladders bend and bounce as Steve and Chris make their regular journeys to and from their straw pile to replenish their supplies. The roof begins to take shape and to look as firm and solid as if it was made from far hardier materials than mere straw. The brothers have their tools beside them as they work. Many go back through the generations; 'In years gone by my grandfather used a milk bottle to get the shape he wanted round some curved parts of the roof. Then eventually he made a rounded, wooden tool specially for the job. He used to work alone but with us its different. Generally Chris starts one side of the roof and I start the other and we tend to meet somewhere near the middle. We don't race one another or anything like that. We go steady and make a proper, neat job of it. And that's the way we like to go on. There's a lot of work now around the villages. We don't have to travel much further than a fifteen to twenty mile radius, which is good for us. We buy all our materials and straw and such in local villages from farmers, whose fathers my grandfather dealt with. And that works really well. One of our important thatching tools is a pair of shears. They're very sharp and we use them for cutting the eaves. One day when I was working, my hair was very long and I said to our Chris; "Ere, come and give me hair a cut". And he came and tried to cut it with the shears, which are as sharp as razors for trimming the straw. But they wouldn't cut my hair, would they? No good at all. And all he did was to take a big chunk out of the back, which gave everyone something to laugh about for a week or two!'

Looking back from the top of the lane the two brothers are silhouetted against the sullen, January sky as they fight to get finished ahead of the approaching storm. Their roof will have to survive twenty years and more of winter gales and storms and summer heat and droughts.

MARK Dixon is a self-employed carpenter from Saxon Leas, Winterslow. Astonishingly, this wooded area was once notable truffle country – those dark delicacies hunted for by pigs in France and by specially-trained dogs in Britain for more than three hundred years. Today, Mark is trying to revive the old skills with the help of his enthusiastic Springer spaniel, Raffles. The best place for truffles is in the beech plantation near to his home but, so far, Mark has not had a lot of success; 'I want to find truffles and there's no reason at all why there shouldn't be truffles here as there was years ago. So far Raffles and me haven't had a lot of luck. But we're both learning still, and we'll get there never you fear. Them days a truffle hunter was thought of as the lowest form of trade. As time went on though, they come up in the world and, like in the thirties, it was quite a sought-after thing. I mean, here in the villages, there was the Collins family and they became quite well-to-do. At least, they always had a pound or two to spend, even though the old chap did die a poor man in the end. But he used to travel round this area and over the Longford Estates and he managed to pick up a lot of truffles and did all right out of it for a while. The truffles must still be here, 'cos the woods are the same and the trees like the truffles just as much as the truffles like to grow under the trees. They both need each other. And the truffles, which are like a dark, firm fungus, like the roots of the beeches. They sort of suckle themselves off those whispy, thin hairs growing off the roots.'

The late afternoon sky is dark and threatening as Mark, slim, dark and tall, marches through the dripping, winter woods with Raffles, handsome, brown and white, and mischievous, scampering at his heels; 'Certainly, the truffles are spread by being eaten by animals and going through them. Pigs used to eat them, of course. But other creatures too. And that's one way they got moved about. Also, a bit like mushrooms, the spores would blow in the wind and then take root that way. I've been interested in the idea of 'em ever since I was a kid. I was born just down the road and I used to come up this way every day on my way to school. I'd always heard about the old days and the Winterslow truffle-hunters and, when I started bringing the dog up here for walks, it just came naturally to try and find 'em. They're grand, old beeches up here. I wouldn't even like to guess at their age. And a few of 'em took a beating from the storms and hurricanes of the last couple of years. Being as most of 'em are still here though, Raffles and I are determined to seek 'em out, so that the Winterslows will be known for their truffles again as they was before the war. I've never seen one, but they're said to be a black, warty, pyramid shape between 30 and 70 centimetres in size. And they lie about 6 inches below the surface, which is where Raffles and his nose comes in. The difficulty is that, as no-one's found one in these parts for 50 years and more, neither Raffles nor I have ever seen one of the things. So what I do is to buy a bottle of truffle essence from the shops. Then I soak bits of bread in it and hide 'em under the trees where I reckon the truffles should be. Raffles finds them OK and digs them up quite well. Like, if he can dig those up, I can't see why he shouldn't find the natural English truffle. His only trouble as a Springer spaniel is that he's a little bit 'gamey'. If a pheasant or a rabbit pops up while we're truffle-hunting he's gone, 'cos he's more interested in chasing things than looking for truffles. But I'm slowly bringing him round – there'd be no trouble at all if truffles had legs and could run!'

As evening draws on Raffles finds, uncovers and devours three big lumps of truffle-scented bread. He is warmly congratulated and is promptly sick. It seems that Mark and his faithful friend still have a long road to travel before they start finding the famous and elusive Winterslow truffles again.

IT is not surprising that a man who lives in Saddlers Cottage, Livery Road, Winterslow, is involved in leather-work. Peter Kingdom began to learn his trade forty years ago. Every kind of job comes his way and his house and workshop are full of his creations and of the rich smell of the leather; 'I was first keen on leather when I was still at school. I used to help the milkman, who drove a horse with a milk-float. I was fascinated over the harness. It was years later that I really got to grips with it but, even then, I could draw pictures of the different pieces of leather with their buckles and write down their names like the milkman told me. And I used to look closely at the harness – how it was made and how it worked and, since then, I've had an abiding interest in leather – all sorts of leather. Of course, horses have come back into fashion now, which is all the better for me and my trade. There are lots here in the village. There's some that graze in the field and others up at the stable. A lot of people have them round here, and they all need some sort of harness one way or another. So I have a fair amount to do for them. But I also like to take on other types of leatherwork – repairing handbags and briefcases, making cartridge belts and boxes, even a sea-chest. Most of the people know me round here and a lot of them bring me things to do.'

Peter is a grey-haired, hospitable man, warmly clothed against the winter wind as he works in a tiny shed behind his cottage. In the dark of a January evening you can see him hard at work through the window, taming, squeezing and sewing the leather, his eyes shrewd, keen and a little tired behind his spectacles. As he toils away a hunting tawny owl floats across the moon and lands softly in a tree at the bottom of the garden; 'I guess there's quite a bit of skill in this work and the hope is that you become more skilful as you grow older. There's nothing that can give you the ability but experience and practice. So, when you reach my incredible age, you should be able to do better and more difficult work than you could when you were younger. At least, that's the theory. It's wonderful to work with leather because it's such beautiful material. You can do many things with it and you can create whatever you want to. And you use different types of leather for all the various jobs you get asked to do. You can mould it and master it just as you wish to. For instance, I'm working on a side-saddle at the moment. It's an unusual looking thing with a lump on the side for the lady to hook her leg over. Side-saddle riding is quite popular in the country, but there aren't many of them round here. So I only get the odd one to work on from time to time. Ordinary saddles are fairly easy to repair, but these ones are a bit more specialised. So it's interesting for me to get this one to work on. Of course, one of the best things about leather is the smell. I come in here in the morning, especially in the summer, and you are surrounded by it. I never tire of that. The other good thing is that it involves a lot of hand-work. In fact, most leatherwork done by saddlers is

Peter Kingdom, surrounded by the tools of his trade which he uses to make saddles and all types of leather work.

101

stitched by hand. A lot of manufactured goods from the factories are machined, but there's still some hand-stitching done even on those. But it's an old tradition up and down the country that much of the saddler's work is by hand. It goes back through the centuries. It takes longer than machine work, of course, but it's stronger, lasts longer and looks better because it's not so uniform. But it costs a bit more too. As for me, I love the trade and wouldn't swap it for anything – nor this part of the world come to that.'

IN the early 1800s, William Hazlitt, that great thinker and author of influential essays, used to lodge at the Winterslow Hut beside the old London Road. He loved these ungainly, hill-top villages and wrote; 'It was in February that I first came here, a willing sojourner, and drank 'wild water' and trod the lengthened greensward by the low woodside. The trees were bare; the groves were silent; and ways were mire. Sharp and sweet it all seemed to me after the dust of London; even the skies seemed new-washed and I felt as if the air cleansed me.'

INDEX

Alvediston 66–67
Annetts, Bill 95–96
Annetts, Chris 95–96
Ansty 11–13

Beaulieu 23–30
Beaulieu Heath 21–30
Beaulieu Motor Museum 25–27
Bentley Wood 94–95
Berwick St John 64, 70
Bishopstone 68–69
Blackmore Vale 9
Bower Chalk 59
Britford 64–66
Broadchalke 67–70
Broadway, John 45–47
Brougham, Peter 39–41
Bulbarrow Hill 9, 14

Case, Maureen 9–11
Cattistock 51
Cerne Abbas 84, 90–93
The Cerne Valley 84–93
Chalk, Dennis 67–68
The Chalke Valley 64–74
Charminster 86–87
Chick, Jim 55–63
Cooper, Brian 80–81

Dixon, Mark 99–100

East Boldre 21, 28–29
East Cholderton 56–57
East Winterslow 94
Ebbesbourne Wake 69–70

Elliot, Guy 75–76
Elsworth, Walter 25–27
Exbury 25

Farleigh 97–99
Flatman, Esmie 47–48
Fox, Dave 87–89
Fry, Robert 69–70

Goodfellow, Cathy 89–90
Goodfellow, Cis 34–38
Goodfellow, Kevin 90
Goodfellow, Vic 33–34
Grant, 'Pay' 66–67

Hardy, Charlie 11–13
The Hawk Conservancy 55–63
Hewlett, Anna 97–99
Hewlett, Chris 97–99
Hewlett, Lionel 97–99
Hewlett, Steve 97–99
Hibberd, Tom 16–19
Hill, Nic 84–86
Holland, Pauline 84–86
Holywell 47
Homington 64
House, Dulcie 13, 14

Keeping, Isaac 28–29
Keeping, Steve 28–29
Kingdom, Peter 100–102
Kitcher, Jeff 23–25

Little London 75–76, 77

Maiden Newton 51
The Melcombes 9–20
Melcombe Bingham 11
The Melburys 43–52
Melbury Bubb 43, 45–47, 49–52
Melbury Osmond 43, 47–49
Melbury Sampford 43–45
Middle Winterslow 94
Miles, Harold 86–87
Miles, Jack 86–87
Miles, Olive 87
Milton Abbas 9–20
Minterne Magna 84–86
Mortimer 77
Muir, David 38–41

Nash, Arthur 78–80
Needs Ore 27
The New Forest 21–30
Nunton 64–66

Oaksford, Bob 48–49

Pamber End 75
Pamber Forest 75–83
Pamber Green 75
Pamber Heath 75
Parfitt, Geoff 94–95
Parsons, David 97–99
Penton, Arthur 64–66
Pickett, John 70–74
Portland 16–19

Ramsdell 80–81
The Rare Poultry, Pig and Plant Centre 10
Rawlings, William 76–77
Raymond, Sheila 14–16

Salisbury 64, 95–96
Saltmarsh 27
Sanger, Reg 41–42
Shaftesbury 48
Sheppard, Molly 90–93
Sheppard, Tom 90–93
Silchester 75
Smith, Ashley 55–63
Smith, Dennis 61–62
Smith, Reg 55–63
Stenhouse, Andrew 49
Stenhouse, Bob 89–90
Stenhouse, Geoff 49
Stenhouse, Mary 89–90

Tadley 75–80, 81–83
The Teffonts 31–42
Teffont Evias 31–42
Teffont Magna 31–42
Tisbury 41–42
Toller Porcorum 51–52
Trollope, Mavis 21–23

Warr, Dawn 43–45
Waterman, Sue 49–51
Webb, John 31–33
Webb, Leslie 68–69
Wessex Shire Park 31–33
West Winterslow 94
Weyhill 55–63
Whaddon 94
Whitcomb, Rosie 51–52
Williams, Jimmy 81–83
Wilson, Graham 27–28
The Winterslows 94–102
Winterbourne Zelston 13
Woodfalls 97–99